The History of Los Angeles

CRAFTED BY SKRIUWER

Copyright © 2025 by Skriuwer.

All rights reserved. No part of this book may be used or reproduced in any form whatsoever without written permission except in the case of brief quotations in critical articles or reviews.

At **Skriuwer**, we're more than just a team—we're a global community of people who love books. In Frisian, "Skriuwer" means "writer," and that's at the heart of what we do: creating and sharing books with readers worldwide. Wherever you are in the world, **Skriuwer** is here to inspire learning.

Frisian is one of the oldest languages in Europe, closely related to English and Dutch, and is spoken by about **500,000 people** in the province of **Friesland** (Fryslân), located in the northern Netherlands. It's the second official language of the Netherlands, but like many minority languages, Frisian faces the challenge of survival in a modern, globalized world.

We're using the money we earn to promote the Frisian language.

For more information, contact : **kontakt@skriuwer.com** (www.skriuwer.com)

Disclaimer:
The images in this book are creative reinterpretations of historical scenes. While every effort was made to accurately capture the essence of the periods depicted, some illustrations may include artistic embellishments or approximations. They are intended to evoke the atmosphere and spirit of the times rather than serve as precise historical records.

TABLE OF CONTENTS

CHAPTER 1: PREHISTORIC BEGINNINGS – THE LAND BEFORE THE CITY

- Formation of Southern California's geography and climate
- Ancient animals and La Brea Tar Pits
  Importance of natural forces in shaping future settlement

CHAPTER 2: THE FIRST PEOPLE OF THE REGION

- Early migration routes and settlement patterns
- Daily life, spiritual beliefs, and cultural structures
- Interaction among local tribes and the environment

CHAPTER 3: THE ARRIVAL OF THE SPANISH

- Motivations for Spanish exploration and colonization
- Early explorers like Cabrillo and Vizcaíno
- Laying the groundwork for missions and future settlements

CHAPTER 4: THE FOUNDING OF EL PUEBLO

- Establishment of the Pueblo de Los Ángeles in 1781
- Role of pobladores and the city's layout
- Struggles, growth, and early governance

CHAPTER 5: MISSIONS AND RANCHOS

- Expansion of mission systems and Franciscan influence
- Native peoples under mission control
- Rise of large ranchos and early cattle economy

CHAPTER 6: THE PUEBLO GROWS AND ADAPTS

- *Increasing population and local governance*
- *Interactions with nearby missions and ranchos*
- *Water management and zanja system*

CHAPTER 7: MEXICAN INDEPENDENCE AND ITS EFFECTS

- *Shift from Spanish to Mexican rule*
- *Secularization of missions and resulting conflicts*
- *Growth of ranchos and early trade developments*

CHAPTER 8: THE AMERICAN CONQUEST

- *War between Mexico and the United States*
- *Treaty of Guadalupe Hidalgo and land transitions*
  Impacts on Californio landowners and native populations

CHAPTER 9: EARLY AMERICAN LOS ANGELES – GROWTH AND CHALLENGES

- *Shifts in governance and local economy*
- *Arrival of diverse settlers and immigrant groups*
- *Law and order issues in a frontier-like environment*

CHAPTER 10: THE GOLD RUSH AND ITS INFLUENCE

- *Role of Los Ángeles as a gateway for gold seekers*
- *Economic booms, migrant waves, and challenges*
- *Social transformations and new trading networks*

CHAPTER 11: RAILROADS AND THE CHANGING LANDSCAPE

- *Expansion of rail lines connecting Los Ángeles regionally*
- *Rise of new towns, land booms, and speculation*
- *Community impacts and the growing power of railroad companies*

CHAPTER 12: THE RISE OF AGRICULTURE AND CITRUS

- *Citrus orchards and cooperative marketing*
- *Irrigation innovations and water distribution*
- *Agriculture's key role in shaping local identity*

CHAPTER 13: EARLY 20TH CENTURY – SHAPING A NEW CITY

- *Population booms and infrastructure demands*
- *Entertainment industry's expansion and film beginnings*
- *Local governance and social shifts*

CHAPTER 14: WATER WARS AND CITY EXPANSION

- *Owens Valley aqueduct controversy under Mulholland*
- *Aggressive annexations and use of water to drive growth*
- *Conflict between urban development and rural communities*

CHAPTER 15: OIL BOOM AND RAPID GROWTH

- *Discovery of major oil fields like Signal Hill*
- *Economic impact and environmental concerns*
- *Rise of new industrial elites and political influence*

CHAPTER 16: HOLLYWOOD AND THE EARLY FILM ERA

- *Founding of major studios and the silent film boom*
- *Creation of celebrity culture and Hollywood's global appeal*
- *Transition to talkies and adaptation of the film industry*

CHAPTER 17: THE GREAT DEPRESSION AND REBUILDING

- *Impact of the 1929 crash, unemployment, and migration*
- *New Deal projects – infrastructure and relief programs*
- *Hollywood's escapist films during hard economic times*

CHAPTER 18: WORLD WAR II AND POST-WAR SHIFTS

- *Defense industry boom and mass migration*
- *Social changes: women in factories, racial tensions, and GI Bill*
- *Post-war economic expansion and suburban growth*

CHAPTER 19: MID-CENTURY DEVELOPMENT

- *Suburban explosion and freeway dominance*
- *Hollywood's golden age, television rise, and youth culture*
- *Early civil rights, environmental, and urban reform efforts*

CHAPTER 20: THE PATH TOWARD MODERN TIMES

- *Watts Riot, Chicano Movement, and social upheaval*
- *Tom Bradley's mayoral victory and inclusive governance*
- *Continuing freeway expansions, environmental regulations, and cultural transformations*

CHAPTER 1

Prehistoric Beginnings: The Land Before the City

Los Angeles did not start as a city. The land itself formed over millions of years, shaped by natural movements and forces. In this chapter, we will explore how the region's hills, valleys, and coasts came into being. We will also look at the ancient creatures that used to roam here, long before people arrived.

The Shaping of the Land

To understand Los Angeles, we first need to picture a time long ago when the world looked very different. During the age of dinosaurs, this area was partly underwater. The shifting of tectonic plates over millions of years pushed up land that would become mountains and hills. California is located on the edge of the Pacific Plate and the North American Plate. These plates still move today, which is why Southern California has earthquakes.

Picture rocky shores rising up from the sea, with waves crashing against them. Picture tall mountains forming in the distance, slowly but surely. This was the scene that set the stage for the land that would one day hold Los Angeles.

Over countless years, water shaped valleys and riverbeds. Rainfall collected in streams that cut across the land. Erosion from wind and water also changed the shape of the mountains and canyons. This gave Los Angeles its varied terrain, from the beaches along the Pacific Ocean to the Santa Monica Mountains and the San Gabriel Mountains further inland.

Volcanic activity may have played a part in forming some of the hills. Lava flows and cooled magma, hidden deep underground, contributed to the region's unique geology. Rocks tell the story of these ancient events. If you look at certain areas, you can find fossils in sedimentary rock layers, showing traces of plants and animals that lived long ago.

Ancient Animal Life

One of the most interesting parts of Los Angeles' ancient past is the presence of big animals. Even though we often think about dinosaurs when we hear "ancient," dinosaurs had already disappeared by the time many of these creatures appeared. Still, the region saw mammoths, mastodons, giant ground sloths, saber-toothed cats, and other large mammals.

These animals lived during the Ice Age, when Earth's climate was much colder. Glaciers covered large parts of the northern continents. Even though Southern California was not covered in ice, the climate here was cooler and wetter than it is now. Many plants grew more easily, and rivers might have been larger, providing water to support big mammals.

A special place called the La Brea Tar Pits, located in what is now central Los Angeles, has preserved many fossils from these ancient animals. Sticky tar seeped out from the ground, trapping animals that wandered too close. As time passed, the bones of these creatures became fossilized, giving us a glimpse of life tens of thousands of years ago. At the La Brea Tar Pits, scientists have found bones of ancient horses, camels, bison, and dire wolves, alongside the famous mammoths and saber-toothed cats.

Early Climate Changes

Climate has always been important to life in Los Angeles. Over thousands of years, the environment slowly shifted from colder and wetter to the warmer and drier conditions we see today. As the Ice Age ended, sea levels rose when the glaciers melted. Many of the big Ice Age mammals either migrated north, changed their range, or became extinct because they could not adapt to the warming weather and shrinking resources.

Different plant communities arose, such as chaparral, oak woodlands, and coastal sage scrub. These are types of plant life that grow well in hot, dry summers and mild, wet winters. Rivers like the Los Angeles River, the San Gabriel River, and others played an important role in shaping human life later on. But these rivers also changed through time. Some would overflow during heavy rainfall, creating floodplains. Others would go dry in years of drought. This pattern continues in the modern age, although we are focusing on earlier times here.

The Importance of Water

In any land, water is key for life. Rivers and wetlands provided drinking water for animals. Where the rivers met the ocean, estuaries formed. These estuaries were rich with fish, birds, and other creatures. Nearby wetlands, marshes, and lagoons hosted countless species that thrived in the mild climate.

Much later, the location of water sources would draw humans to live and build settlements. But, even in the prehistoric era, water shaped the land by cutting paths through rock and soil. It formed canyons and fertile plains. As rain fell on the mountains, streams carried sediment to the lower areas. This sediment created good soil for plants. The cycle of rains and floods left behind natural resources that were important to early humans.

Shifting Landscape and Seismic Activity

Los Angeles sits in a seismically active zone. Earthquakes have always been a part of the region's history. Even in prehistoric times, earthquakes could dramatically change the landscape. An earthquake might alter a river's course, for example, or cause landslides that formed new hills and valleys. While early humans would not have known why the ground shook, they adapted to these events.

These natural changes took place over very long periods. They were not as sudden as events we can see in modern life. But they laid the foundation for what would later become farmland, town sites, and trade routes. The stable or unstable nature of certain areas would, in the distant future, determine where people chose to settle.

Looking Ahead

This chapter gives a glimpse into how Los Angeles' land came to be. By understanding the region's prehistoric beginnings, we see that much of what makes Los Angeles unique is the result of natural processes that took place over millions of years. The fossils and rock layers hold proof of ancient life and shifting climate patterns.

In the next chapter, we will learn about the first human beings who arrived in this land, the people who hunted, fished, and gathered resources from the environment. Their story connects to this chapter because they used the plants, animals, and water sources shaped by all these prehistoric changes.

Additional Exploration of Geological Time

It is easy to forget that the surface of the Earth is constantly changing. We do not see mountains rise quickly, and we do not see valleys form overnight. These things happen very slowly. During the Mesozoic Era (often called the "Age of Reptiles," which includes dinosaurs), the region we now call Los Angeles was largely underwater. If you think about the fossil record from that period, you might find marine fossils where you would least expect them—sometimes high up in hills or mountains. How can this be? It is because the land itself has been pushed upward by the movement of tectonic plates over many millions of years.

As time passed and the dinosaurs vanished (about 66 million years ago), new forms of life flourished. Mammals and birds became more diverse. The climate changed, continents kept moving, and what would become North America settled into its current shape. However, the western edge of the continent remained geologically active because the Pacific Plate rubs against the North American Plate. This boundary is known for the San Andreas Fault, but there are many other smaller faults branching from it in the Southern California region.

Volcanic vents, cracks in the Earth's crust, allowed molten rock to move upward in certain parts of California. In some areas, the magma never broke the surface, and instead cooled underground to form different rock types. Over millions of years, erosion wore away the top layers, revealing interesting rock formations. All these geological events set the stage for the environment that would support human life much later.

Life After the Dinosaurs

After the dinosaurs disappeared, the Cenozoic Era began. This era, which we are still in today, is often called the "Age of Mammals." During the early parts of the Cenozoic, the world was warm and humid. Later, as the Earth's climate changed, ice began to form around the poles. This led to cycles of warming and cooling known as ice ages. During ice ages, large ice sheets covered much of North America. Each ice age ended when the temperature rose again, causing the ice to melt and sea levels to rise.

Southern California, including Los Angeles, was never under a thick sheet of ice. However, the changing climate affected which plants and animals could live here. Sometimes, it was cooler and wetter. Other times, it was warmer and drier, more like the climate we see now. Each shift in climate gave an advantage to some animals and put others at risk. For example, giant ground sloths thrived in cooler, forest-like settings. But as the climate warmed and dried, forests shrank, and grasslands or scrublands took over, which caused problems for animals needing big trees and dense foliage.

Significance of the La Brea Tar Pits

One of the richest sources of fossils from the Ice Age in the Los Angeles area is the La Brea Tar Pits. This site offers a detailed look at what kind of life once roamed here. Many people imagine mammoths as these furry elephants with big curved tusks walking on snowy tundra. However, in Ice Age California, the climate was milder than in places farther north. Mammoths found enough food, such as grasses and other plants, to survive. Saber-toothed cats, with their large canines, hunted animals like bison and ground sloths. Dire wolves, which were a bit larger than modern wolves, also roamed in packs.

The tar pits formed naturally when crude oil seeped upward through cracks in the ground. Much of the lighter parts of the oil evaporated, leaving behind thick tar. Leaves, dust, and water would hide the tar's surface. An animal looking for water or grazing on plants might wander onto this sticky tar and get stuck. Predators smelling fresh prey would come to investigate and sometimes got stuck too. Over time, their bones accumulated in layers of tar. Because the tar is thick and has little oxygen, it preserved the bones very well.

Today, scientists excavate these fossils to learn about the kinds of animals that lived here during the Pleistocene epoch (commonly known as the Ice Age). Studying these fossils helps us understand how the animals interacted with each other, how they responded to climate changes, and perhaps what caused some of them to die out.

Ancient Plant Life and Habitats

It was not only the animals that changed during this period—plants also adapted or moved. The Los Angeles area likely had denser woodlands during cooler, wetter times. Oak trees might have formed broad oak savannas, providing food (acorns) for both wildlife and, later, for people. Chaparral, a type of shrubland, began to spread as the climate became drier. Coastal sage scrub, which grows well in low-rainfall areas, also expanded.

Wetlands and marshes were more common along rivers and near the coast. These wetlands served as stopover points for migrating birds. They also provided habitat for frogs, fish, and insects. Many kinds of plants with shallow roots found perfect growing conditions in these moist areas. Even in a drier climate, these wetlands formed pockets of life that thrived thanks to consistent access to water.

Ocean Influence

The proximity to the Pacific Ocean also shaped the climate. Ocean currents bring cool water from the north down the coast. This is why Southern California gets morning fog or marine layers, especially in coastal regions. Over thousands of years, these ocean currents and air currents have influenced rainfall patterns, temperatures, and storm tracks. Sometimes, warmer water in the Pacific (El Niño events) brings heavier rain, while cooler water (La Niña events) brings drier conditions.

Even in prehistoric times, these patterns likely existed in some form, although not exactly as we see them today. For early people who would eventually come to the region, the ocean provided fish, shellfish, and other resources. Kelp forests off the coast supported marine animals like sea otters, seals, and fish. All of this contributed to an environment that could support human communities once they arrived.

Formation of Important Resources

Besides oil, which we mentioned in connection with the tar pits, the Los Angeles area holds other natural resources. One important resource is clay, found in certain soils, which can be used to make pottery. Early inhabitants would discover this and use it for cooking vessels or storage containers. Another resource is timber from local forests, although large forests are more common in the mountains.

Stone outcrops could be used for tools. In the mountains, people could find stone suitable for making projectile points (like arrowheads or spearheads) and other implements. These resources formed as a result of geological and environmental processes over vast periods. By the time humans arrived, many of these resources were available for them to use, shaping their culture and survival strategies.

Transitioning to Human History

The natural history of Los Angeles set up the conditions that allowed people to live here. The land provided food, water, and raw materials. The climate, while variable, was generally mild. Next, we will examine the arrival of the first people, who might have been drawn by abundant coastlines full of fish and shellfish or the presence of freshwater sources near rivers.

As we move to the next chapter, we will see how these first inhabitants adapted to the land. We will see what they ate, how they built their shelters, and what kind of beliefs they held about the land around them. This is crucial to understanding how Los Angeles first became a place of human settlement. The story of Los Angeles is not just about tall buildings and movie studios. It starts with nature, the movement of tectonic plates, and the rise and fall of ancient creatures, paving the way for the arrival of humankind.

Conclusion of Chapter 1

In summary, Chapter 1 shows us that Los Angeles' history begins with natural forces and ancient life. Mountains, rivers, and plains formed over millions of years. Giant animals roamed the area, leaving fossils in places like the La Brea Tar Pits. The changing climate influenced which plants and animals could live here. Earthquakes and plate movements shaped the land as well. These elements created the foundation that the first people would later use to make their homes.

This foundation is important because it tells us that human history did not appear out of nowhere. It is rooted in geological time and prehistoric ecosystems. Understanding this background helps us appreciate the region's diversity and the challenges people would face living in a place prone to earthquakes and limited rainfall. The next step is to see how the earliest people arrived and managed to live here in harmony with this ancient environment.

CHAPTER 2

The First People of the Region

Now that we have learned about the prehistoric land and animals, let us turn our attention to the first humans in the Los Angeles area. We do not know the exact date when people first arrived, but experts suggest it could have been thousands of years ago, likely during or after the last Ice Age. These early settlers would have found a land rich in resources: a mild climate, abundant sea life along the coast, and diverse plants and animals inland. In this chapter, we explore who these people were, how they lived, and how they shaped the land.

Early Migration to the Region

Archaeologists and anthropologists think that the first people to reach North America likely crossed from Asia over a land bridge called Beringia, which once connected Siberia and Alaska. Over time, these people spread across the continent, forming different groups and cultures along the way. Some eventually reached what we now call Southern California. Because the climate here was comfortable, it encouraged settlement. Rivers, streams, and coastal areas provided food year-round.

It is possible that several waves of migration came into the Los Angeles region at different times. People brought their own ways of hunting, gathering, and making tools. Over thousands of years, these groups learned to adapt to local conditions. They discovered which plants were good to eat, which animals they could hunt, and how to find water sources even during drier seasons.

Early Settlements and Camps

These first inhabitants likely set up seasonal camps. They moved around following the availability of food. For example, in the cooler months, they might stay inland where they could hunt deer or gather nuts and seeds. In warmer months, they might go closer to the coast to fish, collect shellfish, or gather seaweed. This movement made sure they did not exhaust the resources of one single place.

Eventually, some groups became more settled, finding spots that had enough water, plants, and game to support them year-round or most of the year. Archaeological sites show evidence of hearths (fire pits), storage pits, and simple structures like lean-tos made from wood, reeds, or brush. Tools found at these sites include stone knives, scrapers, and arrowheads. These tools tell us about the people's diet and how they lived. For instance, large spear points might indicate hunting of bigger animals, while smaller points might be used for fishing or hunting birds.

Food and Daily Life

Food sources depended on the environment. Along the coast, people relied on fish, shellfish, and even marine mammals like seals if they could catch them. They also gathered kelp and edible seaweeds. Inland, they hunted deer, rabbits, and birds. They gathered acorns from oak trees, which they ground into meal to make a type of mush or bread. They collected seeds, berries, and roots. In the wetlands, they might catch ducks or gather water plants.

Because these people did not have metal tools, they used stone, bone, and wood. They knew which stones made good arrowheads or knives. They shaped these stones by striking them with another rock (known as flintknapping). Bones could be sharpened to make needles, fishhooks, or other small tools. Wood and plant fibers were used for baskets, rope, and shelter materials.

Spiritual Beliefs and Culture

While we do not have written records from these early groups, we can guess that they had spiritual beliefs tied to nature. Many native groups saw animals, plants, and natural forces as part of a larger spiritual world. They might have performed rituals to ensure good hunting or to bring rain. Caves and rock shelters might hold petroglyphs or pictographs—carvings or paintings on rock walls—that tell stories or mark special events.

Family and social structure often revolved around small bands of relatives. People cooperated in hunting, gathering, and child-rearing. Everyone played a part—children might gather berries or learn to make simple tools, while adults took on bigger tasks like hunting and fishing. Elders offered wisdom and teachings based on their experiences.

The Rise of Larger Communities

Over time, as populations grew, some groups began to settle down more firmly. Villages formed around reliable water sources. These villages might have had round houses made from wooden poles covered with brush or tule reeds. People stored acorns in large woven granaries to save food for times when resources were scarce. They also developed trade networks with neighboring groups.

Shell beads became a form of currency. They were made from shells found along the coast, shaped and polished into beads. Inland groups prized these beads, so coastal people could trade them for obsidian (a type of volcanic glass) or other goods not found locally. This trading system tied different tribes together, helping spread ideas and customs.

Specific Tribes of the Los Angeles Area

By the time Europeans arrived centuries later, there were several well-known tribal groups in the region we now call Los Angeles. Two of the main ones were the Tongva (also known as the Gabrieleño) and the Chumash. The Tongva lived in what is now Los Angeles County, parts of Orange County, and the nearby islands. The Chumash lived mainly along the coast north of present-day Los Angeles, including the Channel Islands. There were also other groups in the broader area, each with its own language and traditions.

These groups had different names for themselves, but often Europeans named them after local missions, which is why the Tongva are also called Gabrieleño (after the San Gabriel Mission) and the Chumash near Santa Barbara might be called Barbareño. These terms are not the original tribal names.

Tongva Culture

The Tongva are an essential part of early Los Angeles history. They lived in villages along rivers like the Los Angeles River, San Gabriel River, and Santa Ana River. The name "Tongva" is their preferred modern name, but historically they might have been referred to by other names. Tongva villages had houses made of tule reeds or other plant materials. Inside, people would sleep on mats. Fire pits were used for cooking.

Acorns were very important to the Tongva diet. Women would gather acorns in the fall, remove the shells, and grind the nuts into a fine meal using mortar and pestle. They would leach out the bitter tannic acid by rinsing the meal with water. Then they could cook the acorn meal into a mush or form small cakes. The Tongva also ate seeds from sage and other wild plants, plus berries, roots, and bulbs.

Men often did the hunting and fishing. They made fishing nets from plant fibers, along with hooks and spears. They built plank canoes (called ti'ats) to travel to the nearby islands and along the coast. These canoes were a remarkable achievement, made from wooden planks sewn together and sealed with natural tar. Trade with island communities provided shellfish, dried fish, seaweed, and other marine goods that could be exchanged for acorns, seeds, or game meat from the mainland.

Tongva society had leadership roles, such as a chief (sometimes called a Tomyaar) who guided the village and settled disputes. They also had spiritual leaders or shamans who performed ceremonies. Their religion included dances, feasts, and special rituals. Some of these rituals were for healing, while others were to honor ancestors or natural spirits.

Chumash Culture

Though the Chumash lived primarily in areas north of Los Angeles, their influence reached into parts of the region. They were known for their advanced plank canoes (called tomols), which allowed them to fish and trade extensively among the Channel Islands and coastal villages. Like the Tongva, they ate acorns, seeds, fish, and shellfish, and they also hunted sea mammals like seals and sea otters.

Chumash villages could be quite large, sometimes with hundreds of people. They had a complex social structure, including chiefs, shamans, and craftspeople skilled in making beads and baskets. Their rock art, found in caves and on cliffs, is famous for its bright colors and intricate designs. These paintings often depict swirling patterns and figures that may have spiritual significance.

Interaction Among Tribes

Tribes in the Los Angeles area did not live in isolation. They traded with each other, formed alliances, and sometimes fought over resources. Shell beads from the coast might be traded for obsidian from inland areas, which could be used to make sharp arrowheads. Foods like acorns, fish, and seeds were also exchanged. Coastal tribes might rely on inland tribes for certain meats or plant products that did not grow near the sea, and vice versa.

Cultural ideas, songs, and stories also traveled along these trade routes. Ceremonies and religious beliefs could be shared or influenced by neighboring peoples. In many ways, these early residents of Southern California formed a network of communities, each with its own language and customs but linked by shared environments and resources.

The Influence of the Environment

Just as in prehistoric times, the environment played a big role in how these tribes lived. Droughts could limit water supplies, forcing people to move or adjust their diets. Heavy rains could cause rivers to flood, destroying settlements built too close to the banks. Earthquakes might damage homes or change the course of a stream, which could affect a village's access to fresh water.

Yet these tribes found ways to adapt. They knew how to store food for lean times. They selected building sites with an eye on stability and water access. They observed animal migration patterns and plant life cycles. This allowed them to time their hunting, fishing, and gathering to match seasonal changes. This deep knowledge, passed down from generation to generation, helped them survive and thrive in a land that could be unpredictable.

Early Tools and Technologies

The first people of the Los Angeles region did not have metal, but they were creative with what they did have. They made:

- **Stone tools:** Arrowheads, spear points, knives, and scrapers.

- **Bone tools:** Fishhooks, needles, awls (pointed tools for punching holes), and small knives.

- **Wooden tools:** Digging sticks, handles for stone tools, and frames for houses.

- **Plant-fiber items:** Rope, fishing nets, baskets, mats, and clothing.

Basket-making became an art form in many California tribes. Baskets were used for carrying food, storing goods, and even cooking by placing hot stones inside. The skill involved weaving different materials in tight patterns that could hold liquid without leaking. Every basket design carried meaning, with certain patterns passed down through families.

Sociopolitical Structures

While most tribes did not form large "kingdoms," they had organized village life. A chief might lead several villages or oversee alliances. Tribal councils also existed, where elders could share wisdom. Decisions about wars, trade, or seasonal movements were made through discussions. Traditions and ceremonial practices guided these decisions, as spiritual beliefs were woven into everyday life.

Conflicts could arise over hunting grounds, fishing spots, or other resources. Sometimes villages fought brief skirmishes, but they also formed treaties or marriage alliances to keep peace. Ceremonial gatherings allowed tribes to maintain friendly relations, exchange goods, and celebrate seasonal events together.

Significance in the Bigger Picture

These early groups shaped the Los Angeles area long before Europeans arrived. They managed the landscape through controlled burns (in some cases) to clear underbrush and encourage new plant growth. They established trade routes that would later become paths used by explorers. Their villages often sat in spots with strong natural advantages, such as near riverbanks or at intersections of trails.

By the time Spanish explorers reached Southern California, thousands of native people were living in well-established communities with rich traditions. The Spanish would call them "Indians," but they were distinct tribes with their own identities. These first people set the foundation for human settlement in the area. Their legacy can still be seen in place names, cultural practices, and archaeological sites.

CHAPTER 3

The Arrival of the Spanish

Long before Los Angeles became a bustling city, Spain took notice of California. In this chapter, we will explore how and why the Spanish first arrived in the region, what they saw, and how their coming changed life for the native people. We will look at the main explorers, their journeys, and the early beginnings of Spanish influence that set the stage for a permanent settlement.

1. Spain's Interest in the New World

In the 1500s and 1600s, Spain led expeditions across the Atlantic Ocean to explore new lands. After they reached Mexico and parts of South America, they heard stories about rich lands farther north. Some tales were fantasy, like the myth of a place called "California" full of gold and Amazon-like women. Though these stories were not accurate, they sparked curiosity. Spain wanted to claim as much land as possible to expand its empire, spread Catholicism, and keep other European powers out.

At this time, the idea of sailing along the uncharted coasts of the Pacific was both exciting and dangerous. Ships had to travel thousands of miles from Mexico up the coast, dealing with storms, strong currents, and the unknown. Still, Spanish rulers believed that controlling these coastal lands was important to protect their trade routes. They also feared that rivals, such as the English or Russians, might take over first.

2. Early Spanish Explorers

Juan Rodríguez Cabrillo (1542)

One of the first known European explorers to sail the California coast was Juan Rodríguez Cabrillo, a Portuguese navigator who worked for Spain. In

1542, he traveled north from Mexico in search of new lands. He reached what is now San Diego Bay, then continued up the coast. Although Cabrillo did not fully explore the Los Angeles area or set up any lasting settlement, he recorded notes about the coastline and some of the native peoples he saw from afar.

Cabrillo died during the voyage, but his expedition proved that California's coast was reachable by ship. This was a small but important step in Spain's plan to learn more about the region.

Sebastián Vizcaíno (1602–1603)

Several decades later, Sebastián Vizcaíno led another expedition to map the California coast. He gave Spanish names to various points along the shoreline, including Monterey Bay. Vizcaíno's reports praised California's harbors and resources. He described them as promising places for ports and missions. However, Spain did not act right away. The journey from Mexico to these distant shores was long, and the Spanish empire had limited funds and other priorities at the time.

Still, these early voyages laid the groundwork. They showed that Spain could sail north to California if needed. Over time, small rumors of foreign ships in the Pacific, especially from Russia, pushed Spain to think more seriously about settling the area.

---

3. The Role of Missions in Spanish Plans

Spain believed that the best way to secure California was to build missions and convert native people to Catholicism. Along with missions, the Spanish government would build presidios (forts) to protect them. Over time, small civilian towns might grow near these missions and presidios. This plan was seen as a way to plant Spanish culture in far-off lands and keep other nations out.

A Catholic order called the Franciscans, led by Father Junípero Serra, took charge of building these missions throughout "Alta California." They had already founded missions in Baja California (which is part of present-day Mexico). Now they would move north into what is today the state of California in the United States.

The mission system worked like this: Priests would choose a site with fresh water, good soil, and enough native people nearby to teach and convert. Soldiers from a presidio would guard the mission in case of attacks. Over time, local natives would be brought into the mission, taught the Catholic faith, Spanish language, and European farming methods. The Spanish crown believed this was both a religious duty and a way to increase its power.

4. The Sacred Expedition (Portolà Expedition of 1769)

One of the most important steps in the Spanish occupation of Alta California was the Portolà Expedition of 1769. Gaspar de Portolà was a soldier and the first governor of Las Californias. He led soldiers, settlers, and Franciscan missionaries north from Baja California with two main goals:

1. **Establish missions and presidios** in key coastal areas.

2. **Find Monterey Bay**, which had been praised by earlier explorers like Vizcaíno.

Father Junípero Serra joined this expedition to found the first missions in Alta California. The expedition traveled by both land and sea. Some groups went on ships loaded with supplies, while others walked or rode on mules along rugged trails.

Hardships Along the Way

Travel in 1769 was not easy. The expedition faced hunger, disease (including scurvy), and rough terrain. Because they had limited knowledge of the land, they often ran short on fresh food and water. Mules and horses sometimes died, and soldiers fell ill. Early missions like San Diego de Alcalá were started under these difficult conditions.

Still, the group kept moving north. Along the route, they saw rolling hills, coastal bluffs, and wide valleys. They came in contact with many native groups, who offered fish, seeds, or roasted game to the weary travelers. In some encounters, the Spanish tried to show friendship, giving gifts like beads and small trinkets.

The expedition eventually reached Monterey Bay, though it took time for them to recognize it because Vizcaíno's descriptions seemed different from what they saw. Though the mission in Monterey would be founded soon, the Spanish also took note of the lands in and around what we now call Los Angeles. They saw a promising location by a river that ran from the mountains to the ocean. This would later become crucial in founding El Pueblo de Los Ángeles.

5. First Contact with Native Peoples in the Los Angeles Area

When the Spanish explorers passed through the region that would become Los Angeles, they found villages of Tongva people (later called Gabrieleño by the Spanish). The villagers grew or gathered their own food and had a strong cultural system in place. The Spanish were impressed by the land's resources—clean water, good soil, and mild weather. But they also viewed the native people as potential converts to Christianity.

These early meetings were sometimes friendly. The native people might greet the Spanish with curiosity and offer assistance. In other cases, misunderstandings or fear led to tension. The Spanish carried weapons and sometimes took resources, which alarmed local tribes. Still, the Spanish recorded in their journals that the basin looked ripe for settlement, with plenty of space for farming and ranching.

6. Reasons for Establishing a Settlement in Los Angeles

After the Portolà Expedition, Spanish leaders saw the need for a settlement in the Los Angeles basin for several reasons:

1. **Strategic Location:** The basin was about halfway between San Diego and Monterey. A settlement here could help link missions along the coast.
2. **Natural Resources:** The Los Angeles River could provide fresh water, while the fertile plains were perfect for growing crops and raising livestock.
3. **Native Population:** There were many native villages, which meant missionaries could try to convert and gather them into the Spanish system.

At that time, Spain was also worried about other European nations. If they did not fill the land with Spanish settlers, someone else might.

7. Early Mission Outposts Near the Basin

Before a pueblo (town) was formally founded, missions began to take shape in Southern California. San Gabriel Mission was established in 1771 by Father Serra and others. It was located near the San Gabriel River, which was within traveling distance to the area that would become Los Angeles.

The mission had two purposes: to serve as a base for converting native people and to act as a stepping stone for travelers moving north or south. Soon, it became one of the more prosperous missions in Alta California. It grew grapes and other crops, raised cattle, and welcomed natives who were brought into the mission system. This activity paved the way for more Spanish presence in the region.

---

8. The Mission System and Its Impact on Native Life

The mission system drastically changed native life. When natives joined a mission, they were taught new skills like farming, weaving, and pottery using Spanish methods. They also had to follow strict rules set by the missionaries. The Spanish banned many traditional ceremonies and spiritual practices. Native people who tried to leave a mission without permission were often brought back by soldiers.

Diseases introduced by the Spanish, such as smallpox and measles, also spread through native populations who had no natural immunity. This led to high death rates, causing deep sorrow and disruption to their way of life. Some native people tried to resist the mission system, but the Spanish had weapons and support from the government.

In many missions, natives did most of the physical work—planting fields, tending livestock, and constructing buildings. The Spanish priests oversaw the spiritual teaching and daily operations. Soldiers guarded the missions from possible attacks by hostile groups. Meanwhile, Spain's claim over California tightened as more missions were founded.

9. Political and Military Structure

By the late 1770s, Spain's hold on Alta California included:

- **Missions:** Religious centers run by Franciscans.
- **Presidios:** Military forts with soldiers.
- **Pueblos:** Civilian towns for Spanish settlers.

In theory, a mission would operate for about ten years. After that, it was supposed to become a regular parish church, and the native people would become full Spanish citizens, free to manage their own property. However, in practice, many missions kept going under missionary control for much longer, sometimes decades, because Spain believed it was safer and because the missions' leaders felt the natives needed more guidance.

Los Angeles had not been founded as a pueblo yet, but the Spanish government was eager to get that done. They needed ordinary settlers—farmers and ranchers—who would build homes, grow food, and solidify Spain's control. Missions alone were not enough to demonstrate clear ownership of the land. Real towns were needed.

---

10. Linking to the Founding of El Pueblo

By 1781, the Spanish crown and local leaders were ready to establish a civilian settlement near the banks of the river in the Los Angeles basin. Governor Felipe de Neve, the Spanish governor of California, played a major role in planning this. He outlined how the new pueblo should be organized. The location was chosen for its water, farmland, and strategic value.

The next chapter will focus on the official founding of "El Pueblo de Nuestra Señora la Reina de los Ángeles." We will see who the first settlers were (often called pobladores), how they built the early town, and what life was like in these beginning years. But this chapter ends with a reminder that the arrival of the Spanish set in motion big changes. The land that had belonged only to native tribes for thousands of years would soon become part of a Spanish colonial system. Missions, presidios, and pueblos were about to reshape the region forever.

A Deeper Look at Spain's Motivations

Spain's empire in the 1700s stretched across much of Central and South America, as well as parts of what is now the southern United States. However, many of Spain's territories were thinly populated, and resources for distant colonies were limited. California was on the far edge of the empire. Some Spanish officials questioned whether it was worth the cost to send expeditions there, given the distance and hardships.

But rumors of Russian hunters moving south from Alaska alarmed the Spanish. They also worried the British might try to claim parts of the Pacific coast. Securing California with missions and towns was a way to discourage foreign powers. This competition between European countries was a strong driving force behind settlement. While religious conversion was important, politics and defense also played big roles.

The Journey from Mexico to California

The overland trip from Mexico to California could take months. Travel routes were not well established. The Spanish often followed old native trails. Since the territory included deserts, mountains, and rugged coastline, travelers needed strong animals and enough supplies. The pack animals carried food, tools, seeds, and religious objects for building missions. The Franciscan missionaries usually walked or rode mules, wearing simple robes. Soldiers wore light armor and carried muskets or swords.

At night, the group would set up camp, often near streams. They would post guards to keep watch. Some nights were peaceful. Other times, they faced wild animals or had tense encounters with native groups who did not want strangers passing through. Because these expeditions were large, with dozens or sometimes over a hundred people, they made a strong impression on the local tribes, many of whom had never seen such a large traveling group with horses and cannons.

Challenges of Early Mission Life

Once a mission site was chosen, the Franciscan priests and soldiers would work with local natives to gather materials for building. At first, they often built simple wooden huts with thatched roofs. Later, they might build adobe structures—made from sun-dried mud bricks—because adobe stayed cool in summer and kept warmth in winter.

Inside the mission compound, there was usually a church, living quarters for the priests and soldiers, workshops, kitchens, storerooms, and sometimes a blacksmith shop (though early on, they might not have a skilled blacksmith). Over time, missions also built large corrals for animals, fields for crops, and orchards.

Agriculture was a main goal. Missionaries introduced wheat, barley, grapes, oranges, and other Old World crops to California. They also brought livestock such as cattle, sheep, horses, and pigs. Many of these animals adapted well to the climate. Soon, missions raised huge herds, which changed the landscape. Overgrazing led to fewer native plants, affecting wildlife that depended on them. This was one of the first big environmental changes caused by the Spanish presence in what is now Los Angeles County.

Native Reactions to Spanish Presence

Not all native people welcomed the Spanish. Some were curious about the new animals, metal tools, and beads or clothing the Spanish offered. Others were alarmed by the sudden changes. Many natives tried to keep their own traditions alive, practicing dances and ceremonies in secret. Some groups attacked missions to free their people, but Spanish soldiers often responded harshly.

Over time, a complicated relationship formed. Certain native individuals rose to become leaders in mission life, acting as go-betweens for the priests and the broader native community. Others refused to cooperate. Disease outbreaks, forced labor, and the breaking of old cultural patterns led to high native death rates and much hardship. This shaped a painful chapter in California's history.

Yet, it is important to note that in 1769, everything was still just beginning. The missions had not yet fully taken over the land. Most native villages remained outside direct Spanish control at that point. It would take decades for the mission system to expand and for native populations to feel its full impact.

Father Junípero Serra's Role

Father Serra is a central figure in early California history. He was born in Majorca, Spain, and became a Franciscan missionary. He arrived in Mexico in the mid-1700s and worked in the missions there before being chosen to lead the church's efforts in Alta California. Serra was deeply committed to his faith and believed in saving souls through baptism. He walked many miles despite leg pain and other health issues.

While admired by some for his dedication, many native descendants today see Father Serra's actions in a more critical light, because the mission system undermined native cultures. Still, historically speaking, his leadership was key in founding the chain of missions up the coast of California, including the ones that influenced the Los Angeles region.

The Search for Monterey and Discoveries Along the Way

The Portolà Expedition's main goal was to find Monterey Bay, which was described in glowing terms by earlier explorers. However, when the group arrived, they did not immediately realize they had found it. Vizcaíno's written descriptions did not match perfectly. As a result, the group continued on, reaching the area near present-day San Francisco before returning south.

During this journey, they made detailed notes about the land and the native communities. These notes went back to Spanish officials, who used them to plan future missions and settlements. They learned where fresh water was abundant, which rivers were navigable, and how local tribes lived. Much of the land around Los Angeles was described as having many oaks, grasslands, and a river that flowed most of the year (though it could be dry in summer).

Prelude to a Pueblo

By the late 1770s, a clear decision was made: Spain needed a permanent civilian settlement in the Los Angeles basin. Governor Felipe de Neve drafted a set of instructions called the "Regulations for the Government of the Province of the Californias." These rules covered how new pueblos should be laid out and managed. Neve believed that these towns should not rely too heavily on the missions. Instead, they should have their own municipal governments, with mayors (alcaldes) and councils (regidores), forming the basis of Spanish civil society in California.

The idea was to give land grants to settlers who would farm, raise livestock, and pay taxes to the crown. This was a big step in changing the region's population from mostly native villages and missions to a mix of Spanish, mestizo (mixed ancestry), and other settlers with their own land. Neve's plan would soon come to life in the Los Angeles area.

The French Threat?

While Spain mostly worried about Russia and Britain, there was also some concern about France. France had been active in other parts of North America, such as Canada and Louisiana. If France ever decided to move west, it could pose a problem. Though French ships did not sail near California as often as British or Russian vessels, Spain still saw the need to be prepared. Every European power wanted to grow their colonies and influence. California, with its long coastline and potential for ports, was a valuable prize.

Spiritual Versus Secular Goals

It is important to remember that the missions were not the only Spanish presence. Over time, more secular (non-religious) settlers would come. Some soldiers, once their duty ended, would stay in California. They might marry and become ranchers. Tradesmen, like blacksmiths, carpenters, and tailors, followed the missions to offer services. The missions, presidios, and soon-to-be pueblos formed a network of Spanish life that covered hundreds of miles along the coast.

Yet, in 1769 and the few years after, the missions were the core. Their founders saw Alta California as a place to spread the Catholic faith. The Spanish crown wanted to strengthen its control. These dual motives combined to shape the policies that affected thousands of native inhabitants. Neither the missionaries nor the crown could fully predict how big or complex California's future would become.

Setting the Stage for El Pueblo de Los Ángeles

By 1781, with the founding of San Gabriel Mission already in place, the next logical step was a pueblo nearby. The mission would offer religious support, while the pueblo would attract families to work the land. The Spanish believed that once they had a self-sustaining town, it would secure Spain's hold on the region. It would also reduce the cost of shipping supplies from Mexico if locals produced their own food.

In the next chapter, we will explore exactly how that pueblo was founded, who the settlers were, and what day-to-day life looked like in those very early years. We will learn about the group known as the "pobladores," made up of people from different backgrounds who all came together to build a new community. This moment marks the start of the official story of Los Angeles as a Spanish town.

CHAPTER 4

The Founding of El Pueblo

In Chapter 3, we learned how Spanish explorers and missionaries began to look at the Los Angeles region for settlement. Now, we move forward to 1781, the year El Pueblo de Nuestra Señora la Reina de los Ángeles was officially founded. We will see how Governor Felipe de Neve helped plan the new town, who the first settlers (pobladores) were, and what challenges they faced as they built a community from the ground up.

1. Why Build a Pueblo?

Spain needed a civilian town in the Los Angeles basin for several reasons. First, it was part of a larger plan to populate Alta California with settlers loyal to Spain. Missions alone were not enough to claim the land. Second, the location near the Los Angeles River offered fresh water, farmland, and easy travel routes. Finally, a pueblo could help supply food to nearby missions and presidios, reducing dependence on shipments from Mexico.

Governor Felipe de Neve had already founded a pueblo in San José (in the northern part of California) under rules called the **Regulations for the Government of the Province of the Californias**. He believed that each pueblo should have enough farmland, grazing land for animals, and a central plaza (public square). There would also be a small government structure for overseeing local matters.

2. Choosing the Site

Spanish officials wanted the pueblo near the Porciúncula River, which is what the explorers had named the river (today, we call it the Los Angeles River). The land around this area had good soil. There was also enough open space for grazing livestock. The climate was mild, with light rain in winter and sunny, dry summers, perfect for growing crops like wheat, corn, beans, and chili peppers.

However, the exact spot for the town had to be carefully chosen. Flooding was a concern if the houses were built too close to the river. They also wanted to be near enough to the San Gabriel Mission for support, but not so close that the mission overshadowed the pueblo. Eventually, they picked a location not far from where the river's path was most reliable.

3. The Regulations of 1779

Governor Neve's regulations listed how to set up a pueblo:

1. **Land Grants:** Each settler would receive land to farm, plus a house lot in the pueblo.

2. **Plaza Layout:** The town was to be built around a central plaza. Streets would extend from this plaza in a grid-like pattern.

3. **Water Rights:** The pueblo needed access to a water source, often through irrigation ditches (zanjas).

4. **Town Council:** Over time, the pueblo would form a council to manage local affairs.

Neve believed these steps would help new towns develop in an orderly way. People would have a share of farmland and a clear structure for daily life.

4. The First Settlers (Los Pobladores)

On September 4, 1781, a group of 44 settlers arrived to start the new pueblo. They are often called **Los Pobladores**. These families came from various backgrounds. Some were of Spanish descent, while others were of mixed ancestry (Spanish, African, and Indigenous). This diversity would shape the cultural mix of Los Angeles from the very start.

Each family was given some basic supplies by the Spanish crown, such as:

- Tools for farming (hoes, shovels, axes)
- Seeds for planting crops (wheat, corn, beans)
- Livestock (cattle, sheep, horses)

In return, they pledged loyalty to the Spanish king and agreed to follow the rules set by the colonial authorities. They were expected to build homes, farm the land, and help the pueblo grow.

5. Official Naming of the Pueblo

The full name given to the town was **El Pueblo de Nuestra Señora la Reina de los Ángeles**. In English, this means "The Town of Our Lady the Queen of the Angels." Often shortened to "El Pueblo de Los Ángeles," it honored the Catholic faith and reflected Spain's tradition of long, religious names for new settlements.

Over time, people simply called it "Los Ángeles" or even shorter, "L.A." But in these early days, the mission priests and government officials used the full formal name. Documents from the period often have it written in fancy script.

6. Early Housing and Layout

When they first arrived, the settlers did not have grand houses. They built simple huts or shelters of wood, reeds, or adobe. Adobe bricks, made from mud and straw, became very common once the settlers had time to prepare them. Adobe walls helped keep the interior warm in winter and cool in summer.

The pueblo was laid out around a central plaza. This open area could be used for gatherings, markets, and public events. Over time, a small church would be built, along with a guardhouse (cuartel) for the local soldier detachment. The settlers' homes were arranged in blocks around the plaza, often sharing common walls or fences. As the town grew, more structures would appear along newly formed streets.

7. Daily Life in the New Pueblo

Farming and Ranching: The settlers worked in the fields, planting corn, wheat, beans, and chili peppers. Livestock such as cattle provided meat, hides, and tallow (fat for candles). Horses were important for travel and hauling goods.

Irrigation Ditches (Zanjas): To water the crops, the settlers dug a network of ditches that guided river water to their fields. A man called the **zanjero** was in charge of maintaining these ditches and deciding how much water each field could get. If a ditch broke or got clogged, fields could be ruined by either floods or drought.

Social and Family Life: Families often had many children to help with chores. Children might feed animals, gather wood, or carry water. Women cooked meals, made clothing, and sometimes worked in the fields. Men took on heavier farm work, though everyone pitched in when needed.

Religion and Community: The Catholic Church played a major role. Priests from the nearest mission (San Gabriel) visited often. Religious holidays and celebrations brought the small community together. Over time, a simple chapel would appear in the pueblo itself.

8. Interaction with Native Tribes

From the start, there were native people living around the new pueblo. Some were Tongva who had not joined the San Gabriel Mission, while others were from different villages. The settlers sometimes employed native people for labor, paying them in food, clothing, or small amounts of money. Many natives, on the other hand, resented the loss of their lands and the strict rules of the Spanish system.

Conflicts did happen, though they were not constant. The Spanish crown had laws meant to protect indigenous rights on paper, but in practice, abuse occurred. As the pueblo grew, native land was often taken for farms or grazing. Some natives moved closer to the mission or the pueblo to find work or to seek protection from other tribes. Others stayed away, wary of Spanish influence.

9. Government and Oversight

At first, the pueblo's government was simple. A local leader or alcalde handled day-to-day problems, while the soldiers enforced law and order. For big matters, they looked to the governor, who might live far away, like in Monterey or San Diego. Letters, messengers, or travel by horseback were the main ways to communicate. This meant decisions could take weeks or even months.

Still, the settlers had some local control. They appointed town council members (regidores) to help manage communal lands, water rights, and minor disputes. The laws were based on Spanish colonial codes, which combined church and state authority. It was not a democracy as we know it today, but it allowed some local say in how the town was run.

10. Early Challenges for the Pueblo

Floods and Droughts

Living by a river was both a blessing and a curse. In wet years, the river might swell and flood the fields. In dry years, the water level dropped, leaving crops thirsty. This forced the settlers to work together to maintain the zanjas. A serious flood could damage homes, roads, and farmland.

Disease

Life in the 18th century was harsh in many ways. Common illnesses we can easily treat today, such as flu or bacterial infections, were sometimes deadly. Doctors were rare, and medical knowledge was limited. Outbreaks could quickly spread through the pueblo and nearby native communities.

Limited Supplies

Though the settlers tried to grow or make most of what they needed, certain items like metal tools or fabrics had to come from Mexico by ship or by long caravan. Delays in shipments meant people often made do with homemade solutions. Some settlers specialized in certain crafts—like blacksmithing or carpentry—to help their neighbors in exchange for food or labor.

11. Growth and Community Spirit

Even with these hardships, the pueblo grew. The families who settled here found ways to help each other. They celebrated fiestas on religious feast days, gathered in the plaza for social events, and supported neighbors when crops failed or sickness struck. Over time, new settlers arrived, increasing the population. The pueblo took on its own identity, distinct from the mission.

While the mission at San Gabriel focused on religious conversion, the pueblo aimed at forming a working Spanish community that produced goods. In many ways, the pueblo was also a buffer between the mission and the frontier. Adventurous settlers might push further into nearby valleys to graze cattle, slowly expanding Spain's presence in the region.

---

12. Relations with the Mission San Gabriel

Mission San Gabriel and the pueblo cooperated, but they also competed. The mission had large herds of cattle and fields of its own, which sometimes rivaled the pueblo's economy. The priests wanted the native population to remain at the mission, while the settlers occasionally wanted native labor in town. The Spanish government tried to balance these interests, but tensions arose.

Over time, the mission's wealth grew, thanks to thousands of cattle and the labor provided by converted natives. The pueblo, on the other hand, had to develop its farmland with fewer resources. Still, many villagers found that the mission's church was their closest place of worship, and they relied on the mission's support in spiritual matters and emergencies.

---

13. Daily Food and Cooking

Food in the early pueblo was simple but filling. Corn tortillas, beans, and stews made from local meats (like beef or goat) were common. Chili peppers gave flavor to many dishes. Settlers made bread from wheat flour if they had a mill. Some households grew small vegetable gardens with onions, garlic, squash, and herbs.

Cooking was done over an open fire or in a simple adobe oven. Clay pots were used for boiling and stewing. Meals were often eaten communally, with family and neighbors sharing what they had. Meat could be roasted on spits, and fresh produce was eaten in season. Food preservation methods included salting, drying, or smoking meat for later use.

14. Clothing and Crafts

Most men wore simple cotton shirts, trousers, and sometimes leather jerkins for protection. Women wore long dresses or skirts made of cotton or wool. Finer clothes, if available, were saved for special occasions like weddings, baptisms, or religious festivals. Over time, people in the pueblo also adopted local resources, such as using native plant fibers or animal hides for certain items.

Crafts like pottery and weaving evolved. Some settlers learned from native techniques, while natives who worked for settlers might learn Spanish styles. This blending of cultures is one of the reasons why California later developed unique art and craft traditions.

15. Security and Defense

Though this was not a heavily fortified area, a small detachment of soldiers lived in or near the pueblo. Their job was to protect against horse thieves, smugglers, or hostile raids. Raiders might steal livestock or attack travelers along the roads connecting missions and towns. If a serious threat arose, the pueblo could ask for help from presidios in San Diego or Santa Barbara, though they were quite far away.

For day-to-day security, neighbors often formed patrols to guard cattle herds and watch for trouble. The Catholic Church also had a moral influence. Stealing or harming neighbors was strongly discouraged, though crimes did happen.

16. Childhood in the Pueblo

Children were an important part of daily life. They learned chores early, helping in the fields or watching younger siblings. Schooling was limited at first. Some parents taught children basic reading and writing if they themselves knew how. Otherwise, the local priest or a visiting teacher might offer lessons. Most learning took place at home, focusing on practical skills like farming, cooking, and caring for animals.

Free time was spent playing games, like tag or simple ball games made from leather or cloth. Children might also imitate adults by setting up tiny "farms" with pebbles and sticks, or by "helping" with small chores. As they got older, boys learned hunting, horseback riding, and farming. Girls learned household tasks, weaving, and sometimes how to run small trade, like selling baked goods.

---

17. Festivities and Holidays

Religious feasts were the highlight of the year. The feast day of a patron saint or a major holiday like Christmas brought the whole community together for processions, Mass, music, and dancing. Food was shared, and people dressed in their best clothes. These events helped bind the community together, reinforcing friendships and alliances.

Weddings were also big celebrations. They might last several days, featuring singing, guitar playing, and big meals. Children's baptisms were another reason to gather. These religious milestones were a chance for the pueblo to strengthen its sense of unity and shared culture.

---

18. The Pueblo's Early Economy

At first, the pueblo had a barter system, where people traded goods and services. As it grew, a local economy emerged. Hides and tallow from cattle became valuable exports. Some settlers began to specialize. One family might focus on raising wheat, another on making cheese, another on blacksmithing. Surplus goods could be taken to the mission or to other settlements in exchange for items not produced in the pueblo.

The lack of solid roads or easy trade routes made trading difficult. Goods had to be carried on mules or ox carts over rough tracks. Shipping by sea was easier for large cargo, but the nearest decent port was in San Pedro or San Diego, requiring additional travel.

---

19. Early Conflicts and Resolutions

No community is without conflicts. Sometimes, settlers argued over water rights or property lines. If a field's irrigation ditch was blocked or if livestock trampled a neighbor's crops, tempers could flare. The alcalde (mayor) often tried to mediate. Since the population was small, people had to find ways to get along, or risk harming the entire pueblo's success.

Punishments for crimes might include fines, public labor, or short terms in a small jail. Serious crimes could be referred to higher authorities. The Spanish legal system included some protections for the accused, but it also allowed harsh penalties for those found guilty of certain offenses.

CHAPTER 5

Missions and Ranchos

After the founding of the Pueblo de Los Ángeles in 1781, life in the region began to change. Two major forces reshaped the land and the people: the growth of the **mission system** and the rise of large **ranchos** (land grants) under Spanish (and later Mexican) rule. In this chapter, we will explore these missions and ranchos in detail, looking at how they worked, how they affected native people, and how they set the stage for a new way of life in early Los Angeles.

1. Expanding the Mission System

The Purpose of Missions

We have already learned that the Spanish crown wanted to control and populate Alta California. Missions were one of the main tools for doing this. The **Franciscan order** of Catholic priests, led by figures like **Father Junípero Serra** (in earlier years) and later successors, established a chain of missions. These missions were spaced so travelers could go from one mission to the next without facing a long, dangerous journey alone.

The missions served religious, political, and economic purposes:

1. **Religious:** Convert native people to Catholicism and teach them European practices.

2. **Political:** Assert Spain's claim to the land, preventing other European powers from moving in.

3. **Economic:** Develop agriculture and livestock to support Spanish settlements.

Missions Near Los Ángeles

Several missions were especially important to the Los Angeles area:

- **Mission San Gabriel Arcángel (founded in 1771):** This mission stood closest to the Pueblo de Los Ángeles and heavily influenced its early growth.

- **Mission San Fernando Rey de España (founded in 1797):** Located in the San Fernando Valley, this mission helped shape that region's ranching and farming.

Each mission worked similarly. They brought in native people, taught them new skills, and used their labor to plant fields, care for livestock, and build mission buildings. Over time, these missions became large centers of production, storing foods like wheat, corn, and beans, as well as raising cattle, sheep, and horses.

---

2. Daily Life at the Missions

Buildings and Layout

A typical mission included:

- A large **church** for worship.

- Living quarters for the priests.

- Workshops for weaving, blacksmithing, and carpentry.

- Storehouses to keep grain, tools, hides, and tallow (animal fat).

- Corrals and fields to hold and feed livestock.

Buildings were often made of **adobe**—mud bricks mixed with straw—because adobe stayed cool in the summer and warm in the winter. Red tile roofs helped shed rainwater and protected against sun. Over time, many missions became centers of local architecture, featuring arches, courtyards, and bell towers.

Labor and Routine

Native people, once baptized and living at the mission, did much of the work. Their day usually began with morning prayers and chores. Men worked in fields, tended livestock, or built new structures. Women often wove cloth, made clothing, cooked, and took care of children. Everyone gathered for meals and religious services on a regular schedule. Sundays and holy days included Mass and some rest from heavy labor.

While some natives adapted to mission life, others missed their traditional ways. They had grown up following different beliefs and customs. Mission rules were often strict. Priests and Spanish soldiers kept watch, and natives needed permission to leave. This led to tension and a sense of loss for many indigenous families, who wanted to keep their own cultures alive.

Food and Clothing

Missions aimed to be self-sustaining. They grew crops like wheat, barley, corn, and vegetables. They raised cattle, sheep, and goats for meat, leather, wool, and tallow. This gave them enough basic food and materials. Mission workshops produced rough wool blankets, simple cotton clothing, and leather goods such as saddles.

The Spanish introduced foods like olives, grapes (for wine), and citrus fruits. Over time, these items became part of California's agricultural heritage. Clothing often mixed Spanish styles (cotton shirts, skirts) with local materials. For special occasions, mission leaders might wear more elaborate garments, but most daily outfits were simple and practical.

---

3. The Impact on Native Peoples

Cultural Changes

One of the biggest effects of the mission system was the cultural change forced upon native communities. Spanish friars taught Christianity, the Spanish language, and European customs. Natives were discouraged or forbidden from practicing their own spiritual traditions. As a result, many old dances, songs, and ceremonies went underground or faded away. This caused confusion and sorrow among tribes who were used to living according to their own beliefs.

Disease and Decline

Another serious problem was disease. Natives had little resistance to European illnesses like measles and smallpox. When these diseases spread, many people died. The missions had limited medical knowledge, and with crowded living conditions, sickness could move fast. Over time, entire villages lost much of their population, leading to grief and a major decline in native cultures.

Loss of Freedom

Though some natives found missions useful for stable food and shelter, many felt trapped. Mission rules were strict, and punishments for disobedience could be harsh. Soldiers stationed at the missions could chase after natives who ran away. Families were often separated when children or adults were moved to different missions. The structure of mission life took away much of the independence that native peoples once enjoyed.

4. Rise of the Ranchos

What Are Ranchos?

In addition to missions, the Spanish (and later the Mexican) government granted large pieces of land to individuals. These big plots of land were called **ranchos**. Owners of ranchos, known as rancheros, used the land mostly for raising cattle and horses. In time, these ranchos would become a main source of wealth and power in California.

During the Spanish colonial period, these land grants were not as large or as common. However, after Mexico gained independence from Spain (in 1821), the new Mexican government gave out more ranchos in an effort to boost the economy and reward loyal citizens. We will explore Mexican Independence in a later chapter, but even during the late Spanish era, ranchos began to appear around Los Angeles.

Obtaining a Land Grant

To get a rancho, a person had to petition the governor, explaining why they wanted the land and how they planned to use it. They needed to show they could raise livestock, grow crops, and defend the land if needed. If the governor agreed, the petitioner received a **land grant** document. Once approved, the new owner typically built a small house or ranch house, corralled animals, and hired workers. Over time, some ranchos grew to tens of thousands of acres, creating vast estates.

5. Life on a Rancho

Daily Work and People Involved

Ranchos revolved around **cattle raising**. Cattle provided meat, hides (for leather), and tallow (for making candles and soap). Ranch owners, or

rancheros, hired **vaqueros** (cowboys) to manage the herds. Vaqueros were skilled riders who roamed the land on horseback, herding cattle from one grazing area to another. They watched for strays, branded new calves, and protected the herds from rustlers or wild animals.

Many vaqueros were of mixed Spanish and native heritage. They developed special techniques for riding and roping that later influenced American cowboy culture. Their clothing included wide-brimmed hats (sombreros), leather leggings (chaparreras), and colorful sashes. Life on the rancho could be tough, but for those who loved horses and open land, it offered a sense of freedom.

Rancho Homes and Style

Rancho homes, known as **adobe haciendas**, were bigger than most mission quarters or pueblo homes because landowners often had money from cattle sales. The house might feature a main courtyard, thick adobe walls, and tiled roofs. Some rancheros painted their walls with bright colors or decorated them with simple patterns.

Furniture was often handmade. Tables, chairs, and beds were built from local wood. Floors might be packed earth or brick. A large fireplace served as the cooking area, though many tasks were done outdoors. Rancho families liked to host **fiestas**, or parties, especially for weddings, religious feast days, or branding events. These gatherings could last for days, featuring music, dancing, and plenty of food.

The Economy of Hides and Tallow

Spanish and Mexican California had no big factories, but it had a strong market for cattle products. **Hides** were shipped to other Spanish colonies or even to Europe, where they were turned into saddles, belts, boots, and more. **Tallow** was melted down to make candles and soap. Trade ships came to the California coast, anchoring at places like San Pedro or San Diego. Ranchers traded hides and tallow for items they could not make themselves, such as tools, spices, fine cloth, and sometimes luxury goods like wine.

Because money was scarce, many deals were done through barter. A ranchero might trade a stack of hides for a barrel of sugar and a set of metal tools. This system worked as long as supply and demand were balanced. When too many hides piled up, or when trade ships were delayed, ranchers had trouble selling their goods.

---

6. Relations Between Missions and Ranchos

Sharing Land and Resources

Missions and ranchos existed side by side. Sometimes, a mission would grant part of its lands to a rancher, or the rancher would hire natives from the mission as laborers. In other cases, tension arose because missions claimed large areas for their fields and livestock, leaving less space for private ranchers. Disputes over water and grazing rights could lead to conflict.

Native Labor

Both missions and ranchos relied heavily on native labor. At missions, the friars supervised native workers in farming and building. On ranchos, rancheros often hired local natives to tend livestock, repair fences, or gather crops. Payment varied. Some were given wages, while others received food, clothing, or shelter instead of money. Still, the strict social order often placed native people at the bottom, with fewer rights or freedoms.

7. Social Hierarchy in Early Los Angeles

From the earliest days under Spanish rule, society in California had layers:

1. **Spanish-born officials:** Royal governors and military commanders held top power.

2. **Creoles:** People of Spanish ancestry born in the Americas, sometimes with wealth and status.

3. **Mestizos:** People of mixed Spanish and indigenous ancestry, a large part of the population. Many were vaqueros or small-scale farmers.

4. **Indigenous peoples:** Native tribes or those working at missions and ranchos, often with limited rights.

5. **Afro-Latino individuals:** Some were free settlers, while others faced discrimination. However, in early Los Angeles, there was notable diversity among pobladores and ranch hands.

Rancheros who owned land had a high position. They could influence local decisions, especially if they had large herds or successful crops. Mission priests also held great power, both religious and economic, as they managed large communities and vast resources.

8. Trading, Smuggling, and Foreign Ships

Although Spain wanted to keep strict control over California's coastline, foreign ships—especially from Britain and the United States—sometimes appeared. They traded goods in exchange for hides and tallow. Legally, Spanish law said trade should go through official channels, but **smuggling** did happen. Some ranchers found it easier to exchange goods directly with a foreign captain than wait for approval from faraway authorities.

This underground economy helped rancheros buy items they needed for daily life. It also made them more independent from the missions, which often tried to control local trade. Over time, increasing contact with foreign ships would open California to outside influences, but in these early years, Spanish officials tried to limit it to keep authority in their own hands.

9. Conflicts and Banditry

As more ranches appeared, the wide-open spaces of Southern California gave opportunities for **bandits** or horse thieves. With herds spread across large areas, it was tough to guard every animal. Some men turned to stealing horses or cattle and then selling them to traders far away. Ranchers organized **vaquero patrols** to watch for thieves, but vast distances made it easy for criminals to hide.

In some cases, natives who felt wronged by the Spanish system might steal animals to feed their own families or strike back at missions or rancheros who took their land. Tensions sometimes flared into violence, though large-scale attacks were not as common near Los Angeles as in more remote areas.

10. Transition from Spanish to Mexican Control

Though we will explore Mexican Independence in detail later, it is important to note that near the end of the Spanish era and into the early Mexican era, the mission system started to weaken. The new Mexican government wanted to **secularize** the missions—turning them into regular churches and distributing mission lands to private owners or back to native communities (at least in theory).

At the same time, ranchos grew more common. **More land grants** were issued, making some families very wealthy. This shift accelerated after 1821, but even in the late 1700s and early 1800s, the seeds were planted for a society dominated by ranchos and a dwindling mission system.

11. Cultural Life: Fiestas, Rodeos, and Gatherings

Both missions and ranchos had times of hard work and times of celebration. **Fiestas** (parties) were a big part of life. A mission might hold a fiesta for a saint's feast day or a harvest festival. A rancho might celebrate a family wedding or the **rodeos**, which were roundups of cattle. During rodeos, vaqueros from different ranchos worked together to brand new calves and separate herds. They often ended the day with music, dancing, and big meals.

Music included guitars, violins, and sometimes simple drums or rattles. Dances ranged from graceful waltzes introduced by Europeans to local styles that developed in California. People wore their best clothes—bright shawls, decorated hats, and new boots. These gatherings helped build friendships, settle disputes, and create a shared sense of community.

12. Environmental Changes

Both missions and ranchos had a large impact on the environment. Missions plowed fields and diverted rivers for irrigation. Ranchos allowed huge herds of cattle to graze on native grasslands, which changed plant growth and caused erosion. Over time, wild animals like antelope or grizzly bears found fewer habitats as people and livestock spread out.

Fires sometimes broke out, sparked by lightning or accidental blazes near mission kitchens. With more dried grasses from grazing, these fires could spread fast, damaging the land. Settlers did not always understand local ecosystems, so they introduced plants and animals that reshaped the landscape. This legacy of environmental change started in the mission-rancho era and would continue long afterward.

13. Mixing of Cultures

While missions pushed for Spanish ways, a unique blend of cultures emerged. Native peoples who lived at missions and ranchos influenced cooking, language, and crafts. Spanish settlers brought their traditions in religion, architecture, and agriculture. Afro-Latino settlers contributed their own rhythms, songs, and family customs. This mix created an early **Californio culture** that was neither purely Spanish nor purely native, but something in between.

For example, the Spanish guitar merged with native songs, producing new styles of music and dance. Kitchen gardens might combine Old World herbs (like oregano) with native plants (like wild sage). Spanish words and local native terms mixed together, especially for place names, everyday objects, and ranching vocabulary.

---

14. Decline of the Missions

As the 1700s turned into the early 1800s, the mission period reached its peak, then gradually declined. Several reasons stand out:

- **Reduced Native Population:** Disease and harsh living conditions caused many deaths.

- **Change in Government:** When Mexico declared independence from Spain in 1821, new laws and leaders questioned the power of the missions.

- **Push for Secularization:** Mexican officials believed missions should hand over their land and property to civilian authorities or to the native people themselves.

The missions still existed, but their hold over land and labor started to weaken. This set the stage for ranchos to become more prominent.

15. Growth of Rancho Society

While the missions struggled, ranchos thrived. Wealthy rancheros built bigger homes, expanded herds, and held more influence in local politics. A new social scene emerged around large households, fiestas, and family alliances. Marriages between powerful families connected ranchos across the region, forming a network of influence.

Vaqueros and laborers found steady work, though it was still hard labor. Some natives preferred working for a rancho to living under mission rules. Others ended up caught between two systems—no longer able to return fully to traditional village life, but also never truly accepted as equals in rancho society. This complex mix of freedom and restriction defined early Los Angeles.

---

16. Trade and Influence with the Pueblo

Los Angeles, as a pueblo, also benefited from nearby ranchos. Rancheros brought hides, tallow, and produce to town to trade. Pueblo residents sold manufactured items or offered blacksmithing, carpentry, and other services. Over time, a small market grew in the pueblo's plaza where goods exchanged hands. Some rancheros even built townhouses in Los Angeles to stay overnight during business trips, adding to the pueblo's diversity.

Religious events still connected them to the missions. A ranchero might donate cattle to feed mission workers or to celebrate a saint's feast day. Meanwhile, the mission might trade olive oil or wine for hides from a rancho. Though competition existed, these groups also depended on each other, weaving a tight regional economy.

---

17. Ranchos Under Early Mexican Rule

Even before full Mexican Independence took effect in California, changes in Spain's rule hinted at a new direction. Spanish governors started approving more land grants, partially because they needed local allies to help develop the region. Once independence came, the Mexican government allowed even more **private ownership** of land. This soon outshone the missions as the main economic driver.

Los Angeles became the central town for many ranchos in the surrounding area, as rancheros often traveled there to handle paperwork or get official stamps on their land titles. This process helped the pueblo slowly grow into a more important administrative center.

18. Conflicts Over Boundaries

With so much open land and limited surveying tools, disputes arose over the exact boundaries of a rancho. Some rancheros claimed rivers or hillsides as borders that others also wanted. Fences were rare, so cattle wandered. When calves were born, branding them was crucial to show which rancho owned them. **Branding** became the legal proof of ownership, leading to constant watchfulness.

In times of drought, arguments flared when rivers dried up, and ranchers competed for water holes. Some owners formed alliances, sharing wells or diverting water from creeks. Others fought bitterly, bringing in local officials to resolve disputes. Because colonial and early Mexican law could be slow, many issues were settled by handshake deals or threats of force.

19. The Legacy of Missions and Ranchos in Early L.A.

By the end of the Spanish era and into the early 1800s, missions and ranchos both shaped life in the Los Angeles region. Missions introduced new farming methods, domesticated livestock, and European building styles. They also played a key role in converting and controlling native populations, which had lasting cultural impacts. Meanwhile, ranchos spurred the rise of a cattle economy, influenced social hierarchies, and encouraged more people to move into the countryside.

This system laid the foundation for the region's future wealth in agriculture and land development. Without the missions and ranchos, Los Angeles might not have grown in the same way. However, these benefits came at a steep cost to indigenous communities who lost much of their freedom and way of life.

20. Looking Ahead

In our next chapter, we will focus on how the Pueblo de Los Ángeles itself **grew and adapted** during these times. While missions and ranchos expanded across the countryside, the pueblo also changed, slowly turning from a small settlement of a few families into a busier town. We will see how new laws, leadership, and events shaped the daily lives of the people in the pueblo, and we will prepare for the momentous changes that came with Mexican Independence.

CHAPTER 6

The Pueblo Grows and Adapts

Los Angeles began as a small pueblo in 1781. But after a few decades, life there was no longer the same as when the first 44 settlers arrived. The presence of nearby missions, growing ranchos, and shifting government policies meant the pueblo had to adjust and develop. In this chapter, we will see how daily life, government, and community structures evolved. We will also explore some of the challenges faced by an expanding population with varied backgrounds and interests.

---

1. Population Changes

Families and New Arrivals

When Los Ángeles was founded, the settlers—known as **pobladores**—were few. However, children were born into these families, and new settlers trickled in from other parts of New Spain (later Mexico). Some came seeking land, others followed relatives, and a few arrived to work in or near the pueblo. Over time, Los Ángeles grew from a tiny outpost to a larger community. By the early 1800s, you could find many **mixed-heritage** families that blended Spanish, native, and African roots, forming the early Californio culture.

Some natives moved closer to the pueblo, seeking work outside the missions. Others stayed with the missions but visited the pueblo on business or personal errands. A few ranch owners also built small houses in town for when they needed to handle government matters. This mix of people brought variety in language, customs, and traditions.

Children in the Pueblo

Children in the pueblo had more chances to interact with different cultures than before. They might learn Spanish at home but also pick up native words or phrases from friends. While formal schooling was still rare, visiting priests or private tutors sometimes offered basic lessons in reading, writing, and arithmetic. Most learning still happened in the home or on the job. Girls learned to manage household tasks, cooking, and weaving; boys learned farming, ranching, or crafts.

2. Changes in Government Structure

Alcalde and Town Council

At first, the pueblo was guided by a simple system: an **alcalde** (similar to a mayor) and a few **regidores** (council members). As the pueblo grew, these roles became more defined. The alcalde oversaw public safety, managed disputes, and tried to keep order. Council members discussed land issues, water rights, and community projects like repairing irrigation ditches.

Because the governor might live far away—sometimes in Monterey or San Diego—local leaders had to handle most matters on their own. This gave the pueblo a small measure of independence. They relied on Spanish laws and traditions, but adjusted them to fit life in frontier California.

Influence of the Missions and Military

Nearby missions like San Gabriel still influenced daily life. Priests might ask the pueblo's leaders for labor help or offer food supplies in times of crisis. Soldiers from the nearest presidio (which might be in San Diego or Santa Barbara) occasionally visited or passed through, asserting military authority and helping if there was trouble with bandits or hostile groups. However, the pueblo was largely responsible for its own everyday governance.

3. The Zanja System and Water Management

Importance of Irrigation

The Los Angeles River was vital for drinking, washing, and especially farming. Without enough rain to grow crops year-round, the pueblo depended on a system of **zanjas** (irrigation ditches). These ditches funneled river water to fields and gardens. A key official called the **zanjero** oversaw this system. He made sure ditches were in good repair and resolved arguments over water use.

Flooding sometimes damaged the zanjas, while dry spells forced the town to ration water. Community members learned to cooperate, as water shortages could ruin crops and livelihoods. In times of drought, the pueblo might rely on wells or smaller streams, but this was never as reliable as the main river.

Public Works

Maintaining the zanjas was one of the first forms of **public works** in Los Angeles. The alcalde or the town council could require residents to help clear debris from the ditches or repair breaks. Since nearly everyone depended on irrigation, most complied. This sense of shared responsibility helped tie people together, despite their differences.

4. Building and Architecture

Adobe Houses and Public Buildings

As families grew more prosperous, they replaced their simple wooden or brush huts with more solid **adobe** homes. Adobe bricks, made by mixing mud and straw and drying them in the sun, created sturdy walls. Wooden beams supported roofs covered in clay tiles. These houses stayed cool in summer and warm in winter. Floors might be packed earth, and windows sometimes had wooden shutters instead of glass.

Public buildings also improved. The pueblo built a **juzgado** (town hall or courthouse), a small **jail**, and a bigger **plaza** area for gatherings. These structures were usually grouped near the center of town, making it easy for people to meet for announcements or markets.

Churches and Chapels

While the main mission church stood in San Gabriel, the pueblo started to have its own small chapels. Over time, a dedicated church was built in or near the plaza for local worship. Religious celebrations here included baptisms, weddings, and feast day services. Visiting priests often traveled between the mission and the pueblo to perform these rites.

5. Economic Activities: Beyond Farming

Local Crafts and Services

As Los Ángeles became a regional center, more **craftsmen** set up shops. Blacksmiths, carpenters, and shoemakers found clients among farmers, ranchers, and travelers. Women sold homemade clothing, blankets, or pottery in small markets near the plaza. A handful of taverns or inns catered to visitors. Though the economy was still small compared to later eras, it was growing steadily.

Trade with Ranchos

Nearby ranchos needed tools, cloth, and household goods. In exchange, they brought hides, tallow, and fresh produce to sell or trade in the pueblo. Over time, a simple marketplace formed. Some ranchers or vaqueros arrived on horseback, leading mules loaded with supplies. Others came by ox cart, carrying heavier goods. This regular movement boosted the pueblo's economy and linked it closely to the ranching world outside.

6. Cultural and Social Life

Music, Dance, and Fiestas

Residents of Los Ángeles enjoyed **fiestas** (parties) just as much as ranchers and mission communities did. They celebrated religious feast days and town events like a new alcalde taking office. Music might feature guitars, violins, and voices singing folk songs or church hymns. Dances included European-influenced styles as well as local variations. Everyone in town could gather in the plaza to enjoy these gatherings.

Role of Family and Community

Large families were common. Children, parents, grandparents, and sometimes extended relatives lived together in adobe homes. Neighbors also relied on each other, sharing tools, extra food, or help with heavy work like raising walls for a new house. Disagreements happened, but a sense of unity usually prevailed because survival in a frontier setting required cooperation. Gossip could spread quickly in a small town, so people were mindful of their reputations.

7. Law and Order in the Pueblo

The Alcalde's Role in Justice

Because the pueblo was far from major cities, the **alcalde** had strong influence in resolving local disputes. People might bring cases of stolen property, unpaid debts, or personal arguments to him. He would hear both sides and make a decision based on Spanish law and local customs. Punishments could range from fines to short jail sentences or forced labor for a certain period.

Jail Conditions

The early **jail** was a small adobe building with one or two rooms. Serious criminals might be transferred to a presidio with better guards. However, many minor offenses were handled locally, often with the convict performing tasks like ditch clearing or street repair as a form of repayment. Violence sometimes happened, but overall, the pueblo was not a high-crime area, thanks partly to its tight-knit community.

---

8. Interaction with Missions and Indigenous People

Dependence on Mission San Gabriel

Pueblo families often visited Mission San Gabriel for large religious celebrations, baptisms, or marriages. Sometimes the mission provided seeds, livestock, or skilled labor for big construction projects. In return, the pueblo might offer extra produce or labor during harvest times.

Indigenous People Outside the Missions

Not all indigenous people lived at the missions. Some Tongva villages still existed outside direct Spanish control. These communities interacted with the pueblo as well, trading or working for wages. Conflicts occurred if natives felt cheated or if settlers took more land than agreed. Yet in many cases, they formed a network of mutual help, because the pueblo needed local knowledge of the land, and natives needed goods they could not produce themselves.

---

9. Economic and Social Challenges

Droughts and Disasters

Like any farming town, Los Ángeles had to deal with **weather extremes**. A series of dry years meant less water for crops, leading to food shortages.

Livestock might die from thirst or lack of grass. Flood years, on the other hand, could wash away houses and destroy fields. These hardships tested the pueblo's resilience. Community members often had to pool resources to survive tough times.

Disease Outbreaks

Disease, including smallpox or measles, occasionally swept through the region. The pueblo had limited medical knowledge, relying on home remedies, herbs, and the occasional visiting doctor or military surgeon. Illness could spread quickly when families shared close living quarters, and travelers brought new germs. These outbreaks caused many deaths, disrupting the slow but steady growth of the town.

---

10. Changing Ties to Spain

Weakening Royal Support

By the late 1700s and early 1800s, Spain's empire was strained by wars in Europe and rebellions in its colonies. Resources to support faraway places like Alta California were limited. The pueblo received fewer supplies or soldiers from the Spanish crown. This forced Los Ángeles to become more self-sufficient, relying on local produce and trade rather than shipments from Mexico or Spain.

Rumblings of Independence

Although major events of Mexican Independence happened far south of Alta California, news slowly made its way north. Some citizens of Los Ángeles began to see themselves less as subjects of Spain and more as Californios. Ties to local land and community felt stronger than ties to a distant king. Still, day-to-day life continued much the same until Mexican rule formally took hold in California after 1821, which we will discuss more in a later chapter.

11. Adaptations in Agriculture

New Crops and Techniques

Early settlers mostly grew basic crops like corn, beans, and wheat. Over time, they experimented with **new seeds** brought by traders or introduced from other parts of Mexico. Some tried fruit orchards—peaches, pears, and citrus—finding that the mild climate around Los Ángeles was good for these trees. Irrigation ditches had to be expanded and managed carefully for these crops.

Livestock in the Pueblo

While large-scale cattle herds were more common on ranchos, many pueblo families kept a few cattle, goats, or chickens. This provided milk, eggs, and meat. Some also raised horses for transportation. If a family had surplus eggs, cheese, or produce, they could sell it in the plaza or trade with neighbors, helping everyone diversify their diets.

---

12. Roads and Transportation

Old Trails and New Paths

Travel to or from the pueblo was often slow and difficult. Dirt roads connected Los Ángeles to San Gabriel, San Diego, and Santa Barbara. Heavy rain turned these roads into mud; in droughts, they could be dusty and rutted. People typically traveled on horseback or by mule. Ox-drawn carts carried heavier items. Over time, some residents worked to improve roads by clearing rocks or building crude bridges over small streams.

Interaction with Other Settlements

As the region's population grew, more settlements appeared or expanded. Towns like Santa Barbara, San Luis Obispo, and Monterey served as stops along the **El Camino Real**—the royal road linking missions and pueblos. Traders, government officials, and mission friars traveled this path, carrying news and goods. Los Ángeles was now a key stop in this chain, especially for travelers moving up and down the coast.

13. Family Alliances and Marriages

Strengthening Ties

In a small community, marriages were more than personal choices—they built **alliances**. If the daughter of a local shopkeeper married the son of a rancho owner, that might lead to new business deals or shared projects. Families often arranged such matches to ensure economic security and social standing. The church was involved too, checking that couples followed Catholic guidelines.

Inheritance and Land

When a parent died, land often passed to children. This could split farms or ranch lands into smaller pieces, or sometimes one child inherited most of the property. Because the pueblo was still growing, there was usually room for new homes, but boundary disputes arose if maps were unclear. The alcalde or council might step in to confirm property lines and keep peace.

---

14. Religious Life in the Pueblo

Local Chapels and Priests

While the mission priests were the main religious figures in early California, the pueblo began to have its own **chapels** and occasional resident priests. Weddings, baptisms, and funerals brought people together, reinforcing shared beliefs. Religious festivals honored the Virgin Mary, saints, or local patrons. Streets might be decorated with flowers and banners, and a procession would move through the pueblo, led by a priest saying prayers or blessing onlookers.

Belief and Tradition

Over time, a unique blend of Catholic and local customs developed. Some families continued to quietly honor native practices, mixing them with Christian prayers. Others adapted traditions from Africa or other parts of New Spain. This **mix of beliefs** and celebrations made religious life in Los Ángeles distinct from that of Spain or central Mexico.

---

15. Conflicts and Crime

Bandits and Rustlers

Just as ranchos faced horse thieves, the pueblo sometimes dealt with criminals who stole from local farms or shops. Because official military help was not always nearby, residents formed **posses** or neighborhood watches to catch thieves. In serious cases, they might send word to a presidio for soldiers, but it could take days or weeks for help to arrive.

Personal Disputes

Arguments over land, water, or money were common. Since many families were interconnected, a feud between two people might spread tension among relatives. The alcalde tried to settle these issues quickly. Public fights or insults could end up in court, where fines or public apologies were demanded. Overall, serious crime was not as common as small disputes that reflected the challenges of frontier life.

---

16. Celebrations of Growth

Town Milestones

As Los Ángeles got bigger, residents began to hold small "town celebrations." For instance, if a new public building was finished, the community might gather for a ceremony. If an important official came to visit from Mexico or from the governorship, they would be treated to dances and meals in their honor. These events let people see the pueblo's progress—better homes, a well-kept plaza, and more bustling trade.

Pride in the Pueblo

Over time, the people of Los Ángeles felt proud of their growing town. They boasted about fertile farmland, a flowing river, and the plaza's lively market days. Though they faced hardships, they built strong families and communities. This pride helped hold them together during tough periods of drought, disease, or political unrest.

---

17. Influences from Outside

Foreign Explorers and Traders

As the 1800s progressed, more ships from Britain, the United States, and other nations reached California's coast. Some foreign merchants passed through the pueblo, looking to buy or trade goods. These visitors introduced new items like tea, coffee, or manufactured tools. Curious townspeople might try these goods in exchange for cattle products, produce, or handcrafted items.

Ideas and News

Along with goods, travelers brought **news of the outside world**—wars in Europe, independence movements in Latin America, and technology changes in distant lands. Although the pueblo was far from these events, hearing about them sparked questions about the future. People wondered if Spanish power would wane, and how that might affect their lives in Alta California.

---

18. Growing Conflicts in the Larger Colony

Tension with Governors

Some of the Spanish-appointed governors or Mexican provisional governors clashed with local leaders. They might impose new taxes or demand supplies for the military without paying. Pueblo residents grumbled when forced to give up part of their harvest or herd. Sometimes the alcalde tried to negotiate or protest, but governors held higher authority. These disputes foreshadowed bigger changes to come.

Native Resistance

While many native people lived in missions or worked on ranchos, some resisted Spanish control. They might raid outlying farms or missions to reclaim stolen property or free relatives. The pueblo, with its small militia, had limited ability to handle such attacks. This created fear among some residents, but the raids were not constant or widespread enough to destroy the settlement. Still, tension between natives and settlers remained an underlying issue.

---

19. The Pueblo on the Eve of Change

A Stronger Community

By the early 1800s, Los Ángeles was not a sleepy village anymore. It had more families, better buildings, and a functioning local government. People farmed more land, built sturdier homes, and established social ties through marriage and business deals. The economy, while still modest, was stronger than before. Children grew up with a sense that Los Ángeles was their home, separate from Spain's distant rule.

Preparing for Mexican Rule

Unknown to many day-to-day residents, big changes loomed on the horizon. Mexico was on its way to independence, which would bring a new system of governance to Alta California. Missions might be secularized, giving more land to private owners. Foreign ships could become more common, introducing new products and ideas. The pueblo would have to adapt again, possibly in ways that its founders never imagined.

20. Conclusion and Transition

Los Ángeles in the late Spanish period and early 1800s was a pueblo that had learned to stand on its own feet. The people faced droughts, floods, diseases, and occasional conflict, but their cooperation and growing pride helped them persevere. Missions and ranchos still shaped the wider region, but within the pueblo, a unique community identity was forming—one that would play a big part in the decades ahead.

In the next chapter, we will look at **Mexican Independence and Its Effects** on Los Ángeles and the surrounding area. We will discover how new laws and new leaders changed land ownership, shifted power, and opened the door for further development—or new conflicts. The history of Los Ángeles would soon take another big turn as it moved from being a distant Spanish outpost to becoming part of an independent Mexican state.

CHAPTER 7

Mexican Independence and Its Effects

In the early 1800s, life in Los Ángeles and all of Alta California was still under Spanish control. But events happening far away would soon bring major changes. In 1821, Mexico won its independence from Spain. This had big effects on California's government, economy, and society. In this chapter, we will explore how Mexican rule replaced Spanish rule, how missions were secularized, and how life for the people of Los Ángeles changed during this time.

1. The Road to Mexican Independence

Background in Central Mexico

In 1810, a priest named **Miguel Hidalgo** rang a church bell in the town of Dolores, calling the people to stand up against Spanish colonial rule. This action is known as **El Grito de Dolores**, marking the start of Mexico's fight for independence. Rebels wanted freedom from Spain's control over taxes, trade, and governance. The war lasted for over a decade, with many battles and shifting leaders. Finally, in 1821, Spain recognized Mexico's independence.

When this happened, Mexico became its own country, and Alta California became a territory of Mexico. However, California was far from Mexico City. News arrived slowly by ship or overland. Soldiers in distant presidios sometimes did not even learn of the final victory until weeks or months after it happened.

Effects on Alta California

For the people in Los Ángeles, the change meant they were no longer Spanish subjects. They were now supposed to be Mexican citizens. In practice, daily life continued much the same at first. The same families lived in the pueblo, the same ranchos raised cattle, and the same missions worked under Franciscan priests. Yet, over time, new policies from the Mexican government began to reshape everything.

2. Decline of Spanish Authority

Weakening of the Presidio System

Under Spanish rule, presidios (military forts) dotted the coastline from San Diego to San Francisco. They protected missions and pueblos from foreign threats. But by the time Mexico gained independence, many presidios were already short on funds. Soldiers had not been paid regularly, and supplies were scarce. Mexico, dealing with its own internal challenges, did not send much help.

As a result, presidios lost power. The soldiers stationed there grew fewer in number and had limited influence over the everyday affairs of local pueblos. People in Los Ángeles grew used to handling their own matters. If bandits or conflicts arose, ranchers and townsfolk often formed their own small militias.

Reduction of Spanish Officials

Spanish-born officials who had governed Alta California either returned to Spain or adapted to serve the new Mexican government. Some left, worried about losing privileges they had under the Spanish crown. Others stayed, because they had families and land in California. But overall, the direct link to Spanish rule faded quickly. This allowed local leaders in California to gain more independence.

3. Establishing Mexican Governance

Provincial Leadership

After independence, Alta California became a **Mexican province** (later a department). A governor appointed by Mexico City oversaw the region.

However, the distance between Mexico City and California was still huge. Communication could take weeks or months. Governors had to rely on their own judgment and local support. They often faced shortages of money, soldiers, and supplies, making it tough to enforce policies.

Governors during this period included figures like **Pablo Vicente de Solá** (last Spanish governor) and **Luis Antonio Argüello** (first Mexican governor). They and their successors tried to balance Mexico's rules with the realities of life on the California frontier.

Local Autonomy

Because governors had limited resources, local pueblos gained more say in their own affairs. Town councils, known as **ayuntamientos**, became more important. In Los Ángeles, this council handled water rights, land distribution, and basic legal matters. The pueblo's alcalde (mayor) and regidores (council members) had broader powers than before. They also oversaw local courts and addressed disputes among neighbors.

This system gave Californios (people of Hispanic descent born in California) a stronger voice. Wealthy ranchero families also grew more influential, as they could lend money to the government or provide resources in times of need. Over time, Los Ángeles evolved into a place where local leaders set much of the tone, rather than distant Spanish authorities.

---

4. Secularization of the Missions

Reasons for Secularization

One of the biggest changes under Mexican rule was the **secularization** of the missions. Before independence, missions owned large tracts of land and controlled the labor of many native people. The Mexican government, however, viewed the missions as symbols of Spanish colonial power and wanted to reduce the Franciscan friars' influence. Secularization meant transferring mission lands and authority from the church to civil (non-church) leaders.

Mexico hoped this policy would:

1. **Free native people** from mission control.

2. **Open up mission lands** for ranching and farming by private citizens.

3. **Reduce the power** of the church in politics.

Implementation in California

Secularization did not happen overnight. Laws were passed in the 1820s and 1830s calling for missions to hand over much of their land to the government. In theory, native people who had lived and worked at the missions would receive small plots of land for their own use. The rest of the land might be sold or granted to private owners.

However, the process was often chaotic:

- **Mission property** such as livestock, buildings, and tools fell into disrepair or was taken by opportunists.

- Some **mission friars** resisted giving up their holdings, arguing that natives were not ready to live independently.

- Local officials and wealthy families sometimes **took mission lands** without fairly distributing them to the native people.

By the mid-1830s, most California missions were largely secularized. Mission San Gabriel near Los Ángeles lost much of its land. Native people who had worked there faced an uncertain future. Some remained near the old mission buildings, while others scattered to ranchos or returned to what was left of their ancestral villages.

5. Effects on Native Communities

Loss of Mission Support

Though mission life was strict and often harsh, some native people relied on missions for food and shelter after losing their traditional homes and ways of life. When secularization happened, the missions could no longer care for so many. Livestock and crops dwindled, leaving natives without steady supplies.

Some natives tried to farm on small plots, but they lacked the tools and legal support to secure their new lands. Others became laborers on ranchos, working for low wages or basic room and board. This led to poverty for many, and some turned to petty crime or banditry just to survive.

Displacement and Hardship

Long before the missions, native communities had hunted, fished, and gathered resources across the region. Under Spanish rule, they were forced into missions. After secularization, they were left with few options and little protection from exploitation. Illnesses like smallpox, measles, and cholera also continued to reduce their numbers.

At times, local officials made token efforts to help natives integrate into Mexican society. But the dominant culture saw them mostly as laborers. As a result, many native families faced homelessness, hunger, and loss of cultural identity. This was a tragic outcome of both the mission era and its sudden end.

---

6. Growth of the Rancho System

New Land Grants

During the Mexican period, **ranchos** became the main way land was owned and used in California. With missions losing their hold, the government granted large tracts of former mission land (and other public land) to private citizens who requested it. Individuals seeking a land grant had to:

1. **Petition the governor** with a clear description (often very rough) of the area.

2. **Show loyalty** to Mexico and the Catholic faith.

3. **Agree to settle and improve** the land, usually by raising livestock or planting crops.

If approved, the new ranchero received a **land grant** document. Some grants covered tens of thousands of acres. While a few honest rancheros tried to develop the land fairly, others seized more land than stated or expanded into neighboring areas without permission. Surveys were minimal, and official boundaries were often marked by local landmarks like rivers, large rocks, or big trees.

Influence of Rancheros

As ranchos multiplied, ranchero families rose in power. Their wealth came mainly from **cattle**, which provided hides (for leather) and tallow (for candles and soap). Hides were called "California banknotes" because they could be traded for goods from visiting ships. Ranchero families built larger adobe homes, sometimes called **haciendas**, and held grand **fiestas** where they showed off their status.

In Los Ángeles, many leading citizens owned or were connected to ranchos. Their cattle roamed hills and valleys around the town. They provided jobs for **vaqueros** (cowboys), who managed the herds. Vaqueros, often of mixed heritage, perfected riding and roping skills that later influenced the American cowboy tradition.

---

7. Changes in Los Ángeles Under Mexican Rule

Shift in Local Power

Before independence, Los Ángeles was just a small pueblo with limited influence. By the 1830s, it became more significant as ranchero families around it grew wealthy and used the town for trade and social gatherings. Local officials in the pueblo also gained standing because the Mexican government was far away.

Some rancheros moved into the pueblo part-time. They built townhouses so they could attend council meetings or conduct business. This gave Los Ángeles a livelier social scene. Markets expanded as goods from ranchos—meat, hides, tallow—flowed into the town. Traders, both Mexican and foreign, passed through to buy or sell products.

Education and Culture

Formal education was still rare in Los Ángeles. Wealthy families sometimes hired private tutors. A few small schools popped up, often run by religious or well-educated individuals. But overall, literacy remained low. Most learning happened at home or on the job.

However, cultural activities like music, dancing, and storytelling flourished. **Fandangos** (social dances) were popular. People gathered to play guitars, violins, and drums. They danced the **jarabe**, **son**, or other regional styles. During feast days, religious processions filled the streets, blending Catholic themes with local traditions. This mix created a unique Californio culture that belonged neither purely to Spain nor to central Mexico.

---

8. Trade and Foreign Involvement

Increased Foreign Ships

In the Mexican era, Spanish restrictions on foreign trade loosened. Ships from the United States, Britain, France, and other countries began to visit California ports like San Pedro (near Los Ángeles). They came to buy cattle hides and tallow, which could be made into leather goods, candles, and soap. In exchange, they sold items Californios wanted but could not produce themselves, such as:

- Fabric and clothing

- Metal tools and utensils

- Spices, sugar, coffee, and tea

- Luxury items like fine china or decorative objects

Smuggling and Informal Trade

Officially, Mexico tried to regulate trade and collect taxes. But in reality, local officials often looked the other way, allowing **smuggling** to avoid taxes. Rancheros found it easier to trade hides directly with foreign captains for goods they needed. This "under the table" exchange benefited both sides but deprived the government of revenue.

As foreign captains made more money in California, news spread abroad. Sailors and merchants wrote about the region's mild climate, fertile land, and weak government presence. This set the stage for growing foreign interest in California's future, including interest from the United States.

9. Political Tensions and Leadership Struggles

Rivalries Among Governors

California's Mexican-era governors often faced rivals among the local elite. Some ranchero families backed one leader, while others supported a different candidate. The result was a series of power shifts, with some governors losing office or even being forced out by local uprisings.

Leaders like **Manuel Victoria**, **José Figueroa**, and **Juan Bautista Alvarado** each had periods of influence. Alvarado, for example, declared California a free state (briefly) in 1836, though this status did not last. Such turmoil reflected both the distance from Mexico City and the local elites' desire for more control over their lives.

Los Ángeles as a Political Player

Compared to Monterey or San Diego, Los Ángeles had been a minor settlement under Spain. But during the Mexican era, it grew in size and importance. Some leaders even wanted to make Los Ángeles the capital of Alta California instead of Monterey. Although that did not officially happen until much later, the pueblo's increasing economic and political clout showed the region was changing.

---

10. Rising Conflicts with Native Groups

Raids and Resistance

Many native people, displaced by the missions or cheated out of land, banded together. Some sought to reclaim territory taken by ranchos or the pueblo. This led to occasional **raids** on outlying ranches, where cattle were stolen or ranchers were attacked. Local militias responded, but with wide-open spaces and little centralized control, conflicts flared up from time to time.

Hardships on the Frontier

Most of these raids were small-scale. Still, they created fear among ranchers, who worried about losing livestock or facing violence. Native groups, on the other hand, saw ranching expansion as a continuing threat to their survival. With fewer resources and nowhere to go, many turned to banditry as a way to resist or simply feed their families.

The government in Los Ángeles tried to keep order, but there was no strong military presence. Local ranchers sometimes joined forces and went after native groups, punishing them harshly. These cycles of raids and reprisals left deep wounds on both sides.

11. Rise of Notable Californios

Influential Families

During the Mexican era, certain families rose to prominence, owning large ranchos and holding political offices. Names like **Pico**, **Sepúlveda**, **Verdugo**, **Domínguez**, and **Carrillo** became well-known. They married into each other's families, forming alliances. Their ranchos surrounded Los Ángeles, providing economic stability and social influence. These families shaped the region's destiny by funding public projects, sponsoring celebrations, and lobbying for laws that favored ranchos.

Figures Like Pío Pico

One especially important Californio figure was **Pío Pico**. Born at the San Gabriel Mission, Pío Pico rose to become governor of Alta California. He was of mixed African, native, and Spanish heritage, reflecting California's diverse population. He owned large tracts of land, including the Rancho Paso de Bartolo near present-day Whittier. Pío Pico symbolizes how the Mexican era gave some locally born Californios the opportunity to reach high office and accumulate wealth.

---

12. Social Life in Mexican-Era Los Ángeles

Fiestas and Community Events

People in Los Ángeles enjoyed many social gatherings. **Fandangos** and **rodeos** (cattle roundups) were lively affairs. After the branding of cattle, vaqueros would showcase their roping skills, and everyone joined in feasting and dancing. Music included guitars, harps, and violins, with local songs that combined Spanish melodies and Californio flair.

Religious festivals were also important. The feast day of a patron saint might feature processions, fireworks, and communal meals. Weddings could last several days, involving horse races, bullfights (corridas), and big banquets. Baptisms and funerals were occasions for extended family gatherings, reinforcing social bonds.

Clothing and Daily Life

Mexican-era Californios dressed in a style that blended Spanish traditions with local adaptations. Men wore **cotton shirts**, **calzoneras** (loose-fitting trousers), and often had a **serape** or **poncho** draped over their shoulders. Women wore full skirts, blouses, and **rebozos** (shawls). Wealthier families displayed more elaborate clothing, sometimes with embroidered designs and bright colors.

Daily life included farming, ranching, and household chores. People rose early to tend animals, prepare meals, and handle chores. Children played simple games with homemade toys or practiced riding horses. Education was informal unless a tutor or small school was available. Sundays were for church and rest, and the year was punctuated by feast days, which provided breaks from routine work.

13. Economic Boom and Bust

Hide and Tallow Trade

The economy during Mexican rule depended greatly on cattle. Hides and tallow were the main exports, traded with foreign ships. As demand grew, ranchers expanded their herds, hoping to profit. By the 1830s and 1840s, California was known for its **"Cowhide Coast"**, with thousands of cattle grazing across the land.

However, this trade had ups and downs. If foreign demand slowed or if a particular ship did not arrive, ranchers might be stuck with extra hides. When droughts hit, cattle died in large numbers, causing losses. Ranchers who borrowed money expecting big profits could end up in debt if conditions changed. So while some families grew rich, others struggled to keep afloat.

Urban Growth in Los Ángeles

The pueblo itself benefited from the hide and tallow trade. Merchants opened small shops selling goods that rancheros and vaqueros needed—clothing, tools, and household items. Taverns and inns saw travelers pass through on their way to or from the harbor at San Pedro. Craftspeople made saddles, bridles, and other leather goods. Over time, Los Ángeles had a small but growing middle class of shopkeepers, blacksmiths, carpenters, and artisans, though the rancheros still held most of the wealth and power.

---

14. Pressures from the North: Russian and American Presence

Russian Outposts

North of California, the Russians had established a settlement at **Fort Ross** (in what is now Sonoma County) starting around 1812. Although not immediately close to Los Ángeles, the presence of Russians in California made Mexican officials uneasy. They worried that Russia might expand southward. Efforts to watch or control the Russians fell to the short-handed Californio government, which had few soldiers to spare.

Over time, the Russians focused on the fur trade and did not push far into Alta California. Eventually, they sold Fort Ross in the 1840s, but their brief stay showed how foreign powers saw opportunities on the Pacific coast.

American Interest

American traders and explorers also took note of California's resources. Some came by sea, while others, like **Jedediah Smith** in the 1820s, arrived overland. They wrote about California's mild climate and open lands. These stories spread in the eastern United States. By the 1840s, more American settlers began to appear, dreaming of farmland and economic chances. The Mexican authorities in Los Ángeles tried to keep track of these newcomers, but the territory was large and the government was weak, so controlling immigration was difficult.

---

15. Rising Tensions Leading to the 1840s

Political Instability

The Mexican government in California was never very strong. Governors rose and fell. Some local leaders favored closer ties with Mexico City, while others talked about forming an independent California. Ranchero families protected their own interests, which sometimes conflicted with official policies. Meanwhile, foreign ships kept arriving, bringing new ideas and goods.

Annexation Rumors

By the late 1830s and early 1840s, some American politicians began to express the idea that the United States should one day include California. They believed in a concept called **Manifest Destiny**, the idea that the U.S. was destined to stretch across North America. Californios in Los Ángeles and elsewhere heard rumors about this and wondered if their land might be taken over. Some thought that American annexation could bring stability and more trade, but others feared losing their culture and property to American newcomers.

16. Everyday Challenges

Drought and Flood Cycles

During this period, droughts and floods continued to test the region. When a strong drought hit, the Los Angeles River might shrink, forcing the town to ration water for crops. Livestock on ranchos suffered, leading to smaller herds and less income. When heavy rain returned, floods could damage homes, roads, and the **zanja** system. This cycle made life unpredictable.

Health and Medicine

Medical care was still limited. Local remedies often used herbs and home treatments. Barber-surgeons performed basic procedures like tooth extractions or wound stitching. On occasion, a trained doctor might visit from Mexico or accompany a foreign ship. Outbreaks of diseases like **smallpox**, **cholera**, or **malaria** still caused deaths, since vaccines and advanced medical treatments were rare.

---

17. Social Rules and Customs

Class Divisions

Californio society was divided by class. The wealthy ranchero class lived in big adobe homes, rode fine horses, and held **fiestas**. Middle-class shopkeepers and craftsmen in Los Ángeles worked hard to gain respect and influence. At the bottom, many native people and laborers struggled to make a living. Women usually managed the household and supported social events, but they also held some property rights under Mexican law, which let them own land in their own name.

Honor and Reputation

Honor was a key value among the Californio families. Maintaining a good reputation meant showing generosity, bravery, and courtesy. Insults or slights could lead to duels or feuds. Men prided themselves on **vaquero skills** and gentlemanly manners, while women were expected to be virtuous and hospitable. Gossip traveled quickly in a small society, so people carefully guarded their public image.

18. The Rancho Economy Peaks

Demand for Hides and Tallow

During the 1830s and early 1840s, the hide and tallow trade reached its high point. Yankee trading ships anchored off the coast, collecting hundreds or thousands of hides from ranchos. Rancheros used the money (or trade goods) to expand their homes, throw bigger fiestas, and buy luxury items. This era became romanticized later as the **"Days of the Dons,"** with images of endless fiestas and easy wealth.

Problems on the Horizon

Yet, the economy was built on fragile foundations. Cattle herds depended on open grazing land and steady water supplies. A severe drought or a shift in foreign demand could wipe out a ranchero's wealth. Some rancheros borrowed heavily against future cattle sales, only to be ruined when conditions changed. The entire region's prosperity rested on a single commodity: cattle.

19. Prelude to American Conflict

Growing American Settler Presence

By the early 1840s, more Americans began arriving overland, traveling through the Sierra Nevada or crossing the southwestern deserts. Some Californios welcomed them, seeing them as potential business partners. Others worried that Americans might take over. The newcomers often came with a different culture and government expectations. Tensions sometimes erupted over land ownership or legal rights.

The Bear Flag Revolt and Rising Tensions

In 1846, Americans in the northern part of California led a short revolt known as the **Bear Flag Revolt**, declaring California a republic separate from Mexico. This news quickly reached Los Ángeles, causing alarm among Mexican officials and Californios. Rumors spread that U.S. troops were on their way, and local leaders debated how to respond. While Los Ángeles itself was not immediately taken over, the stage was set for a larger conflict.

We will save the details of the American Conquest for the next chapter. For now, it is enough to note that by the mid-1840s, the relationship between California and the United States had grown tense. Mexico's hold on California was weak, and Americans were becoming bolder.

CHAPTER 8

The American Conquest

By the 1840s, the stage was set for a major shift in California's future. Americans were moving westward in growing numbers, and the United States government had its eye on California. In this chapter, we will see how conflict broke out between Mexico and the U.S., how Los Ángeles got caught in the middle, and how the region eventually fell under American control. We will also explore how local Californios reacted, and what happened to their lands and way of life after the American Conquest.

---

1. Background to the U.S.-Mexican War

Manifest Destiny

Many American leaders believed in **Manifest Destiny**—the idea that the United States should expand across the continent from the Atlantic to the Pacific. By the mid-1840s, the U.S. had already annexed Texas, which had been part of Mexico. Tensions between Mexico and the U.S. ran high, especially over disputed borders in Texas.

Interest in California

American politicians and newspapers called California a land of promise, with a mild climate, fertile soil, and a long coastline. They believed it could offer ports on the Pacific for trade with Asia. Some even feared that if the United States did not act, Britain or another foreign power might seize California. American settlers in California also pushed for protection and recognition from the U.S. government.

---

2. The Bear Flag Revolt (1846)

Northern California Uprising

In June 1846, a group of American settlers in the Sonoma area launched the **Bear Flag Revolt**. They captured a Mexican garrison and proclaimed California a separate republic. Their flag showed a grizzly bear and a star, which later influenced California's modern state flag. Although the revolt was short-lived, it signaled that some Americans were ready to break from Mexican authority by force.

Limited Impact on Los Ángeles

Los Ángeles was far from Sonoma, so news of the Bear Flag Revolt arrived slowly. When local Californios heard about it, many were alarmed but did not expect an immediate invasion. However, the revolt did anger Mexican authorities, who began preparing to defend California more seriously, though their resources and organization were limited.

---

3. The Outbreak of War

U.S. Declaration of War on Mexico

The U.S. Congress declared war on Mexico in May 1846, spurred by clashes along the Rio Grande in Texas. In the months that followed, American military forces arrived by land and sea to target Mexican territories, including California. The **U.S. Navy** sailed up the coast of California, seizing ports like Monterey and San Diego with minimal resistance.

Initial Occupation of Los Ángeles

In August 1846, American troops under **Commodore Robert F. Stockton** and **General John C. Frémont** entered Southern California. They moved into Los Ángeles and declared it under U.S. control. Most Californios in the region were not prepared for a full-scale fight. Some local leaders, like **Pío Pico** (the last Mexican governor of Alta California), fled or tried to negotiate. The Americans set up a small garrison in the town.

4. Californio Resistance

Revolt Against American Occupation

While some Californios accepted the American takeover—believing it might bring stable government or new economic opportunities—others strongly resisted. Under leaders like **José María Flores** and **Andrés Pico**, local Californios rose up in September 1846. They forced the small American garrison to retreat. Los Ángeles briefly returned to Mexican rule as Californios reasserted their authority.

This success, however, would be short-lived. The Americans considered California a prime war objective. Reinforcements and better-equipped troops soon arrived, determined to hold the region.

Notable Skirmishes

- **Battle of Domínguez Rancho (October 1846):** Californio forces defeated a U.S. force near present-day Carson.

- **Battle of San Pascual (December 1846):** Near San Diego, one of the bloodiest conflicts in California during the war.

- **Siege of Los Ángeles (December 1846 – January 1847):** The Americans returned in larger numbers, surrounding Los Ángeles to reclaim it.

---

5. The Capture of Los Ángeles

Return of the Americans

In January 1847, American troops commanded by **Commodore Stockton** and **General Stephen W. Kearny** marched into the Los Ángeles area. They had artillery and more soldiers than before. Californio resistance fought bravely but struggled with fewer weapons and less training.

The Treaty of Cahuenga

On January 13, 1847, **Andrés Pico** (leading Californio forces) and **John C. Frémont** signed the **Treaty of Cahuenga** at a ranch in the San Fernando Valley. This agreement ended most fighting in California. Under its terms, Californio soldiers could go home if they gave up their cannons and promised not to resist further. It was not a formal treaty between nations, but it effectively ended the Californio military resistance in Southern California.

---

6. Consequences of the U.S.-Mexican War

Treaty of Guadalupe Hidalgo (1848)

Although fighting ended in California in early 1847, the war continued in central Mexico for another year. Eventually, Mexico City fell to U.S. forces, and both sides signed the **Treaty of Guadalupe Hidalgo** in February 1848. Mexico gave up vast territories to the United States, including California. In return, the U.S. paid Mexico $15 million and assumed some Mexican debts.

For California, the treaty confirmed that the region was now part of the United States. Article VIII of the treaty stated that Mexican citizens living in these lands could become American citizens and promised to respect their property rights. However, enforcing these promises would prove complicated.

Transition in Los Ángeles

With the treaty signed, Los Ángeles was officially under American governance. Military officials managed the town at first, followed by appointed civilian administrators. Californios who had once been Mexican citizens faced a choice: stay and become Americans, or leave for Mexican territory. Most stayed, but their relationship with the new government was not always smooth.

7. Impact on Californio Landowners

Verifying Land Titles

One of the biggest issues for Californios was **land ownership**. Under Mexican rule, ranchos were granted by the governor, often with rough boundary descriptions. Now, the U.S. government required formal proof of ownership through a **Land Commission**. Rancheros had to hire lawyers, surveyors, and translators to defend their claims. Many spent years in court, paying high fees. Some lost their lands due to legal tricks or mounting debts.

Loss of Large Ranchos

Even families with valid grants often sold portions of their ranchos to cover legal and living costs. Speculators from the eastern U.S. came with cash, buying cheap land from Californios in financial trouble. Over time, many old ranchos broke up into smaller farms or were acquired by newcomers. This shift in land ownership greatly changed Los Ángeles and surrounding areas. The once-powerful Californio class found its influence fading.

---

8. Changes for the Native Population

Continuing Displacement

The American takeover did not improve life for native peoples. The Treaty of Guadalupe Hidalgo largely ignored their rights. American settlers and the new government typically viewed them as obstacles to progress. Laws were passed that allowed forced labor or "apprenticeship" for natives, echoing some of the worst aspects of the old mission system. Many indigenous communities already weakened by mission life and disease found themselves with even fewer protections under U.S. rule.

Further Reduction of Land Access

With Californios losing ranchos, native groups also lost the small measure of informal access they sometimes had to these lands. American courts rarely recognized native claims, and violence against native individuals sometimes went unpunished. This grim situation continued a pattern of marginalization and suffering for the original inhabitants of the region.

9. Life in Post-Conquest Los Ángeles

Military Presence and Order

During the first few years of American rule, the U.S. Army kept a watchful eye on Southern California. Army outposts and volunteer militias tried to maintain law and order in a place that was still getting used to a new government. Banditry and horse theft still occurred, especially since many ranchers were struggling to adjust. Some notorious outlaws, like **Joaquín Murrieta** (though his story is partly legend), became symbols of resistance—or criminality—depending on one's viewpoint.

Formation of Civilian Government

As time passed, American officials began to set up civilian government structures. **Town councils** changed, adopting American-style governance. English started to appear in official documents, though Spanish remained common, especially among Californios. Over time, Los Ángeles would transition to become an official U.S. city in the new state of California (1850), but for now, it was a mix of older Californio customs and new American rules.

10. Cultural Clashes

Language and Customs

Californios who stayed in Los Ángeles had to adapt to American culture. Official records, property deeds, and court proceedings were increasingly in **English**. Schools, when they emerged, taught in English. Many Californios only spoke Spanish, creating barriers to full participation in the new system. Meanwhile, Americans often did not bother to learn Spanish, causing misunderstandings and resentment.

Religious Shifts

The Catholic Church continued to serve the spiritual needs of many Californios. However, Protestant churches began to appear as more Americans arrived. Conflicts over church property or religious holidays sometimes arose, though the biggest disputes tended to revolve around land and politics rather than faith. Still, the cultural landscape shifted as more non-Catholic settlers came to live in Los Ángeles.

---

11. Discovery of Gold in 1848

Gold Rush Impact

Only days before the Treaty of Guadalupe Hidalgo was officially signed, gold was discovered at **Sutter's Mill** in Northern California. The **Gold Rush** that followed (starting in 1848–1849) changed California overnight. Although Northern California saw the biggest immediate impact, thousands of people from around the world began passing through or settling in the state.

For Los Ángeles, the Gold Rush created new **trade opportunities**. Ranchers sold meat and produce to gold seekers heading north. Some Californios went to the gold fields to seek fortune. Others stayed in the south, trying to keep their ranchos or adapt to the changing market. The sudden arrival of miners and adventurers also shifted political and social dynamics. By 1850, California was admitted to the Union as a state, cementing American control.

---

12. Reactions of Leading Californios

Figures Like Pío Pico

Pío Pico, who had been the last Mexican governor, tried to protect his wealth and land claims under American rule. Despite his efforts, he faced lawsuits and debts. Over time, he sold much of his property to cover legal fees. Many other notable Californios followed a similar path. They tried to adapt but found the legal environment and economic pressures stacked against them.

Resistance or Cooperation

Some Californios rebelled in small ways or resented the new order, but open resistance faded once the war ended. A few found ways to cooperate with American officials, serving in local government or partnering in business. For instance, some formed alliances with American ranchers or merchants, learning English and navigating the new system. However, the old Californio dominance was largely gone.

13. Changes in Daily Life

Newcomers and Businesses

The American Conquest opened the door for more foreigners to move in. Some started **general stores**, **taverns**, or **hotels** in Los Ángeles. Blacksmith shops and carpentry businesses expanded to meet the demand of growing populations. Transportation also improved gradually as roads were built or widened to handle wagons and stagecoaches.

Shift in Labor

With the ranchos breaking up and new forms of property ownership taking hold, many Californios and native people sought wage labor in or near town. They might work on smaller farms, in vineyards, or in construction. Others continued as **vaqueros**, but the large open range system was slowly changing as private land boundaries became more defined under American surveying.

14. Early American Administration

Military to Civil Governance

For a short time after the conquest, military governors ran California. Then, as part of the treaty, a civil government began forming. Los Ángeles eventually elected **mayors** and **city councils** under American law. English-speaking officials arrived, sometimes clashing with local Spanish-speaking residents. Disagreements over taxes, property deeds, and legal procedures were common.

Introduction of American Law

American laws on property, commerce, and crime replaced or overlapped with the old Mexican code. For people used to the Mexican legal tradition, these new laws could be confusing. Some older customs, like community water rights and grazing on open land, did not fit neatly into the American system of private property. Over time, the courts sorted these disputes, but often to the benefit of those who understood and could pay for the American legal process.

---

15. Banditry and Social Order

Rise of Outlaws

The tension and uncertainty of the transition allowed some individuals to turn to **banditry**. Figures like **Tiburcio Vásquez** became famous (or infamous) for robbing stagecoaches or ranchos. They sometimes claimed they were fighting for poor Californios who had been cheated, but authorities saw them as criminals. The new American system tried to establish regular law enforcement, but wide distances and sparse settlements made policing difficult.

Vigilantes and Community Justice

In response to crime, some American settlers formed **vigilante groups**, taking the law into their own hands. This led to lynchings and extrajudicial punishments. Californios often saw these actions as biased against them, fueling more resentment. Over time, official sheriffs and courts got stronger, but the early years of American control were marked by considerable lawlessness.

16. Cultural Shifts Accelerate

Language and Education

As more American families settled in Los Ángeles, English-language schools and newspapers appeared. Spanish was still spoken widely, but official records and government documents shifted to English. Children from Californio families who wanted to succeed under the new system had to learn English, while American children rarely studied Spanish. This accelerated a cultural shift in the younger generation.

Architecture and Town Layout

Adobe buildings were still common, but new wooden structures or brick buildings began to appear, reflecting American architectural influences. Streets were widened or re-aligned to match American city planning. Over time, Los Ángeles would adopt an urban grid system, though some older Spanish layouts remained in place, especially around the original plaza.

17. Economic Changes After 1850

Statehood and Its Influence

California became a U.S. state in 1850, only two years after the war ended. This quick transition brought more federal attention and resources. Railroads, when they eventually arrived (later in the 19th century), would speed up development. But in the immediate years after 1850, Los Ángeles was a modest town, growing but still struggling with its identity between the old Californio ways and new American influences.

Shifts in Land Use

After the Gold Rush, agriculture diversified. Some Americans introduced **wheat farming**, **vineyards**, and **citrus orchards**. Still, cattle ranching remained important for a while, especially for feeding the growing population. However, repeated droughts in the 1850s and 1860s led to massive cattle die-offs, further weakening the ranchero class. Over time, land passed into the hands of American or European immigrants with new business models.

---

18. Legacy of the American Conquest

Transformation of Power Structures

The American Conquest ended the Mexican era in Los Ángeles. Californio families, once dominant, found themselves in a new society that favored American laws and customs. Some adapted and stayed influential, but many lost their lands and status. Natives suffered further displacement. Meanwhile, American settlers laid the groundwork for a rapidly changing economy that would one day make Los Ángeles a major metropolis.

Lasting Cultural Influence

Despite the upheaval, **Californio culture** left a permanent mark. Spanish place names, adobe architecture, and traditions like rodeos and fiestas carried on. Over time, a new identity emerged that blended American, Mexican, and older local traditions. This unique mix still shapes Los Ángeles' cultural life in many ways.

19. Everyday Adjustments

Fashion and Daily Routines

American-style clothing slowly became more common, though many Californio women continued wearing long skirts and rebozos, and men often kept their traditional hats and sashes. Over time, city dwellers saw simpler, mass-produced items arrive in stores, changing the way people dressed and the types of household goods they used.

Religion and Festivities

Catholic churches remained central to many families' spiritual life. However, new Protestant churches opened, attracting some of the American settlers. Religious festivals continued, but the large-scale Californio fiestas started to decline as ranchos broke up and new social norms took hold.

20. Conclusion and Transition

The American Conquest was a turning point for Los Ángeles. It ended the Mexican era, introduced new laws and customs, and accelerated cultural and economic changes that would shape the future city. Once the dust settled, Los Ángeles remained a small town for a while longer, but the seeds of modern development were planted.

- **Land Ownership:** Shifted from large ranchos to more fragmented properties under American legal rules.
- **Population Growth:** Increased with both American arrivals and global immigration spurred by the Gold Rush.
- **Cultural Mix:** The older Californio traditions blended with new American influences, creating a distinct identity.
- **Legal and Social Changes:** Courts, language use, and governance structures all changed rapidly.

In the upcoming chapters, we will look at how Los Ángeles navigated the **early American period**—including the Gold Rush's ripple effects, the arrival of the railroads, the rise of agriculture and citrus, and other developments that led the city toward its later transformations. For now, the story has reached the point where Los Ángeles has officially become part of the United States, marking the end of one historical era and the start of another.

CHAPTER 9

Early American Los Angeles: Growth and Challenges

When the United States took control of California in the mid-1800s, Los Angeles entered a new chapter. It was no longer a small Mexican pueblo. It was now part of a young U.S. state, with new laws and people shaping its future. In this chapter, we will look at how Los Angeles grew under American rule, what problems it faced, and how the city slowly changed from a dusty frontier town into a busier community.

1. Becoming Part of the United States

Statehood in 1850

After the U.S.-Mexican War ended in 1848, California officially became part of the United States. Just two years later, in 1850, California became a state. Los Angeles was then recognized as a city within Los Angeles County. This was a quick transition. Other territories took longer to become states, but California's **Gold Rush** (more on that in the next chapter) drew so many newcomers that the federal government rushed to admit it as a state.

For Los Angeles, statehood brought both excitement and uncertainty. The city had fewer than 2,000 residents at the time. They had to figure out how to live under new laws, speak a new language (English) in legal matters, and deal with new types of officials. Mexicans who stayed in the region became American citizens almost overnight, although they often faced legal and cultural barriers.

Early American Administration

At first, military governors ran California. But once statehood was granted, civilian leaders took over. Los Angeles elected its own **city council** and **mayor**. The city council handled local issues like roads, water distribution, and public order. Because many longtime residents spoke Spanish, council meetings might include translations. Over time, English gained ground as the official language of city documents, causing tension among Spanish-speaking Californios.

2. Population Changes

Arrival of American Settlers

After 1850, more Americans began moving into Los Angeles, hoping to start farms or open businesses. They came from states like Missouri, Illinois, and New York, looking for fresh opportunities. Some passed through on their way to the goldfields in Northern California. Others stayed, seeing potential in the region's mild climate and open land for agriculture.

These newcomers usually spoke English, dressed in American-style clothing, and followed different customs than the older Californio families. This led to both cultural exchange and conflict. Some Californios felt that the Americans disrespected local traditions, while some Americans viewed the Californios as stuck in old ways. Even so, trade and marriage between these groups slowly formed new connections.

Immigrants from Other Countries

Besides Americans, people came from Europe, Asia, and Latin America. Some German and French immigrants opened shops or practiced trades like blacksmithing and baking. A small number of Chinese immigrants arrived, often first landing in San Francisco, then traveling south. These Chinese newcomers sought work building roads, working in vineyards, or doing laundry. They later formed small neighborhoods in and around the city. Each group added new foods, languages, and customs to the mix.

3. Early City Governance

The First City Charter

In 1850, Los Angeles adopted its first **city charter**, which laid out how the city would be governed. It allowed for a mayor, a council, and local courts.

The mayor oversaw city departments (though they were small), while the council passed local laws (ordinances). Officials were often inexperienced with American law, so they learned on the job. Sometimes, they simply adapted old Mexican rules to fit American guidelines.

The city had only a handful of **police officers** and relied on volunteer or makeshift law enforcement. Small jails were built of adobe, where prisoners awaited trial or short sentences. Justice could be harsh in those days, especially if vigilante groups took matters into their own hands. It took time for a stable legal system to develop.

County Organization

Around the same time, Los Angeles County formed, covering a large area of Southern California. County officials managed issues outside the city limits—things like ranching disputes, tax collection, and overseeing roads between towns. As more settlers arrived, the county had to create new districts and hire sheriffs to maintain order. Los Angeles, as the county seat, served as the center of government for the region.

---

4. Economy in Transition

From Ranching to Farming

During the Mexican era, the local economy revolved around large **ranchos** raising cattle for hides and tallow. Under American rule, many ranchos broke up or were sold when landowners could not prove their legal titles in American courts. Some rancheros kept smaller pieces of land and switched to **farming** crops like wheat, corn, or beans. Others sold out and moved away or took other jobs.

Slowly, more **diverse agriculture** emerged. Small farmers grew vegetables, fruits, and grapes. A few ranchers started sheep herds, selling wool to growing markets. This variety made the local economy more stable than relying only on cattle. However, repeated droughts still caused problems by killing crops and livestock.

Rise of Small Businesses

As new people arrived, local businesses appeared. Blacksmith shops, general stores, carpentry shops, and taverns catered to travelers and residents. Some families opened small hotels for visitors passing through to northern goldfields. A local printing press published newspapers in both English and Spanish, sharing news and advertising local goods. This slowly turned Los Angeles into a small but active commercial center.

---

5. Transportation Woes

Roads and Stagecoaches

In the early 1850s, roads around Los Angeles were rough dirt paths. Traveling to San Diego or San Bernardino took many hours, if not days, on horseback or by wagon. Stagecoach lines were set up to connect Los Angeles with Northern California, though the journey was long and dangerous. These stagecoaches carried mail, passengers, and sometimes gold shipments. Robberies by bandits could happen on lonely stretches of road.

Farmers and ranchers used **ox carts** and horse-drawn wagons to bring produce into town. Muddy roads in the rainy season slowed travel, while in summer heat, dust coated everything. Improving roads cost money the city did not always have. As a result, local leaders often asked merchants or residents to donate labor or funds to fix major routes.

The Port at San Pedro

Los Angeles did not have a deep-water harbor. Ships anchored off **San Pedro**, then used small boats to ferry goods and passengers ashore. Bad weather sometimes forced ships to stay out at sea, delaying deliveries. Many locals dreamed of building a better port, but it would take years to raise enough money. In the meantime, San Pedro remained the main entry point for imported goods, from clothing to farming tools. Merchants then hauled cargo by wagon about 20 miles inland to Los Angeles.

6. Social Life and Culture

Blending of Traditions

Los Angeles still showed strong **Californio** traditions. Families held fiestas for weddings, baptisms, and saints' days. Music often combined Spanish guitar styles with tunes brought by American settlers. Some Americans joined these celebrations, while others kept to themselves. Over time, new forms of recreation emerged, such as American-style dances and Fourth of July festivities.

Families who had lived in the area under Spanish and Mexican rule usually spoke Spanish at home. American newcomers introduced English in schools and businesses. This bilingual environment caused confusion at times but also led to a unique mix of languages. Churches remained important. The **Catholic Church** served many older families and some newcomers, while **Protestant churches** appeared to serve mostly American arrivals.

Fashion and Daily Life

People wore a mix of clothing styles. Californios still dressed in **sombreros**, **rebozos**, and embroidered jackets, while Americans wore broadcloth suits, bonnets, and simple cotton dresses. A day's routine involved farm chores, household tasks, or shop work. Children had few schools, so learning might come from private tutors or church classes. Families spent evenings sharing stories, playing music, or hosting neighbors for a meal. Sundays remained a day of rest and worship.

7. Law and Order Challenges

Crime and Vigilantes

Los Angeles gained a rough reputation in the 1850s for **crime and violence**. Conflicts flared over land, gambling, or racial tensions. The small local police force could not handle every problem. Sometimes, vigilante groups formed to punish suspected criminals without a formal trial. This caused fear and anger, especially when innocent people were targeted.

Banditry was also an issue. Horse thieves or stagecoach robbers took advantage of the region's wide-open lands. Figures like **Joaquín Murrieta** and **Tiburcio Vásquez** became legends, though stories mixed fact and myth. Some said these bandits were folk heroes standing up for poor Californios. Others saw them as outlaws hurting honest residents.

Efforts to Establish Justice

City officials tried to set up courts and jails that followed American legal procedures. However, many judges and lawyers came from other states and did not understand local customs. Translators were needed for

Spanish-speaking witnesses. Trials were sometimes slow or unfair, causing frustration. Still, as the decade went on, better structures for justice took shape. Gradually, a stronger sense of law and order replaced the early chaos.

8. Water Struggles and the Zanja System

The Lifeblood of the City

Los Angeles relied on the **Los Angeles River** for water. Canals or ditches, called **zanjas**, carried water to fields and homes. The city had a water overseer, or **zanjero**, who managed water flow and made repairs. Because of droughts, floods, and limited budgets, keeping these canals working was tough. If the river ran too low, crops died. If it flooded, canals washed out, leaving parts of the city dry.

Conflicts Over Water Rights

As more settlers arrived, competition for water grew. Farmers upstream wanted to divert water for their crops, while those downstream needed enough for their fields and livestock. Fights broke out over who had the right to build new ditches. The city council tried to set rules, but enforcement was weak. These water troubles set the stage for bigger disputes in later years, when the city would seek new water sources elsewhere.

9. Ethnic Tensions

Conflicts with Chinese Immigrants

Chinese workers who arrived in Los Angeles faced discrimination from both Americans and Californios. They often took low-paying jobs or did work considered too dirty or dangerous by others. Some lived in small "Chinatown" areas near the downtown plaza. Businesses run by Chinese immigrants included laundries, produce stands, or small shops selling imported goods.

Tensions sometimes exploded into violence. One of the most tragic events was the **Chinese Massacre of 1871** (which, though slightly later than this chapter's focus, began to develop from the prejudices formed in earlier years). During that riot, a mob attacked and killed several Chinese residents. Anti-Chinese feeling was strong among certain groups who blamed immigrants for taking jobs or lowering wages.

Relations with African Americans

A small number of **African Americans** came to Los Angeles, both as free individuals and sometimes escaping slavery from other states. California was technically a free state, but laws and attitudes were complicated. African Americans faced prejudice, limited voting rights, and difficulty in finding decent work. Still, some managed to start churches or small businesses, adding another layer to the city's diversity.

Native Communities

Native people, displaced during the Spanish and Mexican eras, found little relief under American rule. Missions had been secularized, but many natives did not receive promised land. Some lived on the edges of ranches, working as laborers. Others tried to gather in small settlements near the river. They often faced disrespect and violence. American courts rarely recognized native claims, continuing a tragic pattern of marginalization that started years before.

---

10. Public Health and Safety

Diseases and Medicine

Medical knowledge was limited. Los Angeles saw outbreaks of **smallpox**, **measles**, and other diseases. With little sanitation, wells and ditches could be contaminated. Doctors were few and often trained through apprenticeships rather than formal schools. People relied on home remedies, herbs, or folk cures. Some families could not afford medical help at all.

When epidemics struck, entire neighborhoods might be quarantined, or families would stay at home to avoid infection. The city council sometimes set up temporary hospitals or asked local churches to care for the sick. Mortality rates were high, especially among children. Over time, the city began to develop small clinics and better sanitation rules, but that was slow to take shape.

Fire Risks

Most buildings in early Los Angeles were made of **adobe** or wood. Fire was a constant danger. Oil lamps or open fireplaces could ignite a blaze. Firefighting was primitive—buckets of water, a small volunteer fire brigade, and maybe a hand-pumped engine. Large fires could destroy blocks of the city and threaten farmland. This reality encouraged some buildings to be made of adobe, which did not burn as easily as wood.

11. The Growing Role of Religion

Catholic Church Continuity

The **Catholic Church** remained significant in daily life, especially for Californio families. The old Plaza Church (La Iglesia de Nuestra Señora la Reina de los Ángeles) continued to hold Masses, baptisms, and weddings. Priests sometimes reached out to newer arrivals, though language barriers existed. Many Americans were Protestant, so separate churches were established for their services.

New Denominations

Protestant congregations—Methodist, Baptist, Presbyterian—set up meeting halls or small churches in the city. Missions from these denominations tried to spread their faith. They also ran schools or charity programs. This variety of churches was new for a place used to a single dominant faith. Over time, religious diversity became a normal part of Los Angeles, though the Catholic Church still had a deep historical presence.

12. Newspapers and Information

Early Press

Newspapers began printing in Los Angeles soon after statehood. Some papers published in Spanish, others in English. A few were bilingual, trying to serve both communities. They covered local politics, land cases, crime reports, and shipping news from San Pedro. Ads promoted stores, taverns, or traveling circuses. These papers helped shape public opinion, though their reach was limited by low literacy rates.

Spread of News

Before telegraphs or railroads, news traveled slowly. People learned about national events (like east coast elections) weeks after they happened. Local gossip spread faster, often by word of mouth. Public notices, such as auctions of rancho lands or city council announcements, were posted outside government buildings. Community gatherings also allowed speakers to update people on important changes.

---

13. Notable Early Figures

Benjamin Davis Wilson (Don Benito)

One of the early American settlers who became influential was **Benjamin Davis Wilson**, called Don Benito by Californios. He married into a Californio family and eventually served as a local leader, including as mayor of Los Angeles. Wilson ran a ranch and later helped develop areas like the San Bernardino Valley. Streets and places still carry his name today.

Andrés Pico and Pío Pico

Although Pío Pico and his brother Andrés Pico were well-known from the Mexican era, they remained important in early American Los Angeles. Pío Pico tried to adapt to the new society by investing in businesses and real estate. Andrés Pico served in local government roles. They both struggled with land lawsuits, reflecting the broader problem of Californios losing property after the American takeover.

14. Education Efforts

Early Schools

Formal schools were rare. Some families hired private tutors or sent children to **mission schools** where priests taught reading, writing, and arithmetic in Spanish. After statehood, American teachers opened small classrooms that taught in English, though many Californio parents worried their children would lose their Spanish. As the population grew, the city council voted to fund public schools, but money was tight. Schools often had to collect small fees from families.

Language Barriers

Children of mixed backgrounds sometimes became bilingual, translating for parents or neighbors. This gave them a special role in a city that needed both Spanish and English to function. Over time, more families saw the value of learning English to succeed under American rule, though some wanted to keep Spanish alive at home and in church.

---

15. Small Booms and Busts

Vineyard and Wine Production

In the 1850s, Los Angeles was actually known for its **vineyards**. Mission grapes grew well in the sunny climate, and some residents made wine for local and regional markets. Ranchers replaced old cattle pens with grapevines, hoping for good profits. But the market was small and subject to fluctuations. A disease outbreak or a drop in demand could wipe out a vineyard's income.

Financial Instability

Because the city's economy was still fragile, banks were rare and money was often in short supply. People used gold or silver coins, or they bartered goods. Paper currency from out of state might not be accepted. Small "booms" happened when travelers came through with gold from the north, spending it on supplies. But busts followed if travelers left or if harvests failed. This unstable economy forced many to live with caution, ready to handle sudden changes in fortune.

16. Policing and the Sheriff's Office

Growth of Law Enforcement

By the late 1850s, Los Angeles tried to organize a more formal **law enforcement** system. The city appointed a marshal (similar to a police chief), while the county had an elected **sheriff**. They employed small squads of deputies to patrol roads and watch for thieves. This helped reduce the worst crime, but with a large county area and few roads, banditry still occurred. At least it was now clearer who had the official job of keeping peace.

Jails and Courts

The city maintained a simple jail, often made of adobe or brick. Trials took place in small courtrooms or even in a large home if no official building was available. Judges tried to follow California's new legal codes, but local tradition sometimes overrode formal rules. Over time, more standard American-style courthouses appeared, and the legal process became more orderly. Still, corruption and favoritism were problems, as in many frontier towns.

17. Leisure Activities

Rodeos and Horse Racing

Rodeos were still popular, reflecting Californio traditions of rounding up cattle, branding calves, and testing riding skills. Americans joined in, sometimes bringing their own racing horses. People would gather on weekends to watch or place bets. Winners gained fame for their horsemanship. These events blended older Spanish practices with new American forms of competition.

Gambling and Saloons

Many men in early Los Angeles enjoyed gambling halls or **saloons**. Card games like **faro** or **poker** drew crowds. Drinking could lead to fights, which caused city leaders to worry about public safety. Over time, laws were passed to limit gambling or require licenses, but enforcement varied. Saloons remained a central part of social life for some, while churches tried to discourage "vices" like drinking and gambling.

18. Conflicts Over Ranch Lands

Court Battles

Many Californios spent years in court proving ownership of their ranchos. Boundaries were vague, marked by rivers, hills, or old oak trees. American judges demanded detailed surveys. Lawyers and surveyors cost money. If a ranchero lost, they might have to sell part of their land to pay legal fees. This pattern broke up the old ranchos, creating smaller farms that newcomers purchased.

Transformation of the Landscape

As land changed hands, new owners built fences, divided fields, and introduced crops or new livestock. This marked a shift from the wide-open range of the Mexican era to a more "American" style of property use. Fewer large cattle herds roamed freely, and more land was devoted to wheat fields, vineyards, or orchards. The city's outskirts slowly became patchworks of different farms.

---

19. Moving Toward the 1860s

Political Growth

By the end of the 1850s, Los Angeles had a more stable city council and a few improved roads. Small political parties formed, reflecting national debates of the time. The looming **Civil War** in the eastern United States would also have an impact on California. Though Los Angeles was far from the battlefields, its politics and economy felt the tension. Some residents, especially those from Southern states, sympathized with the Confederacy. Others supported the Union.

Preparing for Future Development

In this period, Los Angeles was still a rough frontier community, but seeds of future growth were planted. Immigrants were arriving, farmland was expanding, and local businesses were finding their place in the larger state economy. The biggest changes were yet to come—railroads, bigger ports, and new industries would soon reshape the city. But for now, the city still depended on dusty roads, the zanja water system, and old adobe buildings.

CHAPTER 10

The Gold Rush and Its Influence

The discovery of gold at Sutter's Mill in Northern California in 1848 changed the entire state in a matter of months. While most of the goldfields lay hundreds of miles away from Los Angeles, the **Gold Rush** still had a huge effect on this growing city. In this chapter, we will look at how the rush for gold shaped the economy, population, and daily life of Los Angeles. We will also see how new routes of travel and trade brought people from all over the world through the region, forever altering its path.

1. The Spark of the Gold Rush

Sutter's Mill Discovery

In January 1848, just as the U.S. and Mexico were finalizing the Treaty of Guadalupe Hidalgo, a worker named **James Marshall** found gold flakes in the American River at **Sutter's Mill** near Coloma in Northern California. News spread slowly at first, but by the end of 1848 and into 1849, the "Gold Fever" drew people from across the United States and even from foreign lands like China, Chile, Australia, and Europe. They were called **Forty-Niners**, referencing the year 1849.

Initial Doubts in Los Angeles

Many residents in Los Angeles, especially Californios who had heard tales of gold before, were skeptical at first. They had known local stories of gold in the hills but never saw large fortunes. When travelers began rushing north, buying supplies and heading through Los Angeles, the city realized this was something new. Soon, Los Angeles merchants stocked mining tools, clothing, and canned goods for sale to fortune-seekers on their way to the goldfields.

2. Population Movements

Southern Routes to the Goldfields

Because Los Angeles was located far to the south, many Forty-Niners who arrived by sea at San Pedro or San Diego still had hundreds of miles to travel over land to reach the gold region. Some who came by land from Mexico or the American Southwest passed through Los Angeles to resupply. This made Los Angeles a "gateway" of sorts, even if it was off the main path from San Francisco or Sacramento.

Horseback, mule trains, and wagon caravans clogged dusty roads. Locals saw new faces daily—people from other states speaking English, or foreigners speaking French, German, or Chinese dialects. This constant flow of people brought money to local businesses but also caused strain on lodging, food supplies, and law enforcement.

Temporary Boom in Town

Some Forty-Niners stayed briefly in Los Angeles. They might rest, repair wagons, or work odd jobs to earn extra cash before moving on. This caused a **short-term boom** in housing rentals and store profits. Taverns and gambling halls also thrived as travelers spent money on entertainment. While most continued north, a small fraction stayed for good, liking the climate or spotting business chances.

---

3. Rising Demand for Food and Supplies

Farms and Ranches Benefit

All those miners needed **food, clothing, and tools**. Northern California could not supply enough at first. So farmers and ranchers in Southern California sold cattle and produce to traders who shipped or hauled it north. The price of **beef** soared. Some ranchers sold entire herds for gold dust or coins. They became richer if they managed to avoid drought or disease in their livestock. This boosted the local economy, though it also encouraged overgrazing and risked environmental damage.

Merchants and Freight Companies

Merchants in Los Angeles stocked shovels, pans, boots, and tents for miners. Freight companies used wagons or pack mules to carry goods up the old Spanish trail or across desert routes. They charged high fees, making good profits. This trade network tied Los Angeles more closely to the rest of California. Although the city still lacked a great harbor, it became an important supply center.

---

4. Social Impacts of the Gold Rush

Diversity of Newcomers

The Gold Rush was one of the first large-scale migrations of people from all over the world to California. In Los Angeles, visitors from Peru, Chile, China, France, Germany, and other places mingled with Americans and Californios. Some traveled on to the mines, while others opened small businesses in Los Angeles when they realized they could profit from selling supplies, running inns, or providing services.

This diversity brought new languages, foods, and customs. Local restaurants might offer Chinese-style dishes or Chilean empanadas. Bakeries sold French bread, and tailors sewed clothing in the latest American fashion. While tension existed, the presence of many nationalities also gave Los Angeles a more cosmopolitan feel compared to its earlier days as a small pueblo.

Rise in Crime and Conflict

The flood of gold seekers also brought **lawless elements**. Some folks spent all their money in gambling halls, then turned to theft. Highway robbery of wagons carrying gold or supplies became more common. The small local police and volunteer militias struggled to cope. Vigilante actions sometimes flared, leading to hangings or beatings without formal trials. Race-based fights also happened, as Americans and foreigners clashed over business or personal insults.

5. Changing Ranching Economy

Golden Opportunities and Risks

For rancheros near Los Angeles, the Gold Rush seemed like a dream. Cattle that once sold for a few dollars suddenly fetched much higher prices as beef. Ranchers used the profits to build bigger homes, host lavish parties, or invest in vineyards. This was a short-lived golden period, though. If a rancher borrowed money and the cattle market crashed, they could lose everything.

Overgrazing and Environmental Impact

To meet the sudden demand for beef, ranchers expanded their herds. They let animals graze across wide open lands, sometimes beyond their rancho boundaries. This led to **overgrazing**, damaging local grasses and soil. Drought years, which were common in Southern California, worsened the situation. When the rains did not come, thousands of cattle starved. By the late 1850s, some ranchos were in financial ruin from these cycles of boom and bust.

---

6. Transportation Improvements

Stagecoach and Freight Routes

With the Gold Rush, the government and private companies paid more attention to **roads** in and out of Los Angeles. Stagecoach lines increased, carrying mail and passengers at a faster pace. Freight companies financed road repairs to speed up deliveries. While roads were still rough by modern standards, they improved enough to handle heavier traffic. This cut travel time to the north or east.

The Butterfield Overland Mail

One notable route was the **Butterfield Overland Mail**, which started in 1858. It ran from St. Louis, Missouri, across Texas, then through El Paso and

Arizona to California. Portions passed near Los Angeles. This mail service helped link the city with the rest of the country, bringing letters and packages more quickly. Though it was discontinued at the start of the Civil War (1861), it showed that Los Angeles was now an important node in American westward travel.

7. Influence on Local Businesses

Blacksmiths, Carpenters, and Crafts

As more travelers passed through, local blacksmiths had steady work fixing wagon wheels, horseshoes, and mining tools. **Carpenters** built crates for shipping supplies north or repaired stagecoach stations. Craftspeople found new markets for leather goods, hats, and boots. This growth in skilled trades allowed some families to build savings and expand their shops.

Hotels and Saloons

Hotels and boarding houses sprang up to serve migrants. **Saloons** multiplied, offering liquor, card games, and sometimes lodging. Bars were not only places to drink; they served as makeshift social clubs where travelers exchanged news and locals heard stories of gold strikes up north. This lively environment created more jobs but also stirred moral concerns among church leaders, who worried about drinking, gambling, and other vices.

8. Shift in Population Center

Northern California Dominance

While the Gold Rush gave Los Angeles a boost, Northern California saw a much bigger effect. Cities like San Francisco exploded in size, becoming the main gateway to the goldfields. San Francisco's deep-water port welcomed ships from around the world, overshadowing smaller ports like San Pedro. Sacramento and Stockton also grew as launching points for miners heading into the Sierra Nevada foothills.

Los Angeles, in comparison, remained smaller and more rural. However, the city's population did climb steadily. By the early 1860s, Los Angeles had grown beyond its original boundaries, with new adobe or wooden houses rising on the outskirts. The city council tried to keep up with demands for roads, schools, and policing.

Influence on Politics

State politics also shifted. Newcomers in Northern California shaped laws that sometimes favored mining regions or the San Francisco port. Los Angeles leaders had to lobby hard in the state legislature to get attention for their needs. This north-south divide in California politics remained a theme for many years, though the Gold Rush period put it into sharp focus.

---

9. The Temptation of Mining

Los Angeles Residents Heading North

Some locals, both Californios and American settlers, left Los Angeles temporarily to try their luck in the mines. They hoped to strike it rich. Few found big fortunes. Most returned empty-handed or with just enough gold dust to buy new land or goods. Still, stories of a lucky strike or a friend who found a nugget kept hope alive.

Local Gold Discoveries

Though overshadowed by Northern California's goldfields, small gold deposits were found in Southern California too—places like the **San Gabriel Mountains** had minor rushes. Some prospectors panned local rivers or streams. But these smaller finds never matched the bonanza up north. They did, however, draw a handful of extra settlers who stayed in Los Angeles when the local mines ran dry.

10. Cultural Changes in Daily Life

Goods and Fashion

With gold wealth circulating around California, finer goods appeared in Los Angeles shops. Miners who struck it rich wanted nice clothing or imported luxuries, like French wines or fancy furniture. Shopkeepers began to stock these items. Women's dresses displayed new fabrics and styles from the East, while men sported fashionable hats or suits if they could afford them. The gap between the rich and poor sometimes widened, as not everyone profited from the boom.

Entertainment

Miners passing through spent money on **theater shows**, dances, and gambling. Traveling entertainers, like magicians or musicians, performed in saloons or rented halls. This introduced new forms of leisure to the city. Californio families also kept their traditional **fiestas**, but now they might invite wealthier Americans or foreign merchants to join. The city's social mix kept expanding.

---

11. Law and Order During the Rush

Increased Crime

With money changing hands quickly, outlaws found opportunities to rob wagons or hold up travelers. Certain roads became notorious for bandit attacks. Local authorities struggled to keep up. Sometimes, Wells Fargo shipments of gold passed near the city, attracting thieves. Robbers hid in canyons or brush, striking when shipments were poorly guarded.

Attempts at Better Policing

In response, Los Angeles tried forming stronger patrols. Ranchers sometimes guarded roads near their lands. The city council discussed building better jails and hiring more deputies, but funding was limited.

Vigilante groups occasionally took justice into their own hands, hanging suspects without trial. This caused fear and divided public opinion. Over time, the city learned that a formal, well-trained police force was necessary, but that would come gradually.

12. Banking and Finance

Early Banks

Before the Gold Rush, there were no formal banks in Los Angeles. People kept gold or silver at home or with trusted merchants. As gold from the north passed through, a few entrepreneurs started "banking houses," where miners could store gold dust in exchange for notes. These early banks helped stabilize local commerce but also faced risks—robbery, dishonest agents, or sudden deposit withdrawals. Some banks failed, while others grew into established financial institutions.

Credit and Loans

Ranchers and merchants sometimes took out loans secured by land or cattle. Banks charged high interest, seeing the frontier as a risky place. If cattle prices fell or a drought hit, borrowers might lose everything. Land foreclosures became more common. This process accelerated the **breakup of large ranchos**, as banks or land speculators took over properties when owners defaulted.

13. Racial Tensions Intensify

Treatment of Mexican and Californio Residents

American newcomers often viewed Spanish-speaking residents with suspicion, especially if they lived in rural areas rumored to harbor bandits. Some Californios wore their traditional outfits, which Americans considered old-fashioned. Many struggled with the English language, making them targets for fraud or unfair deals. Land disputes added to the resentment, as courts seemed to favor English-speaking claimants.

Anti-Chinese Sentiments

Chinese immigrants who passed through or stayed in Los Angeles were met with growing hostility. They were seen as competition for jobs or as outsiders who refused to "assimilate." Despite the vital role Chinese laborers played in building infrastructure (like roads or irrigation ditches), prejudice ran deep. Laws limiting their freedoms or extra taxes on Chinese businesses became more common, planting the seeds of future violence.

Native Peoples Overlooked

Native communities, already devastated by mission times, found themselves further ignored or pushed aside during the Gold Rush. Some tried to work in the city, but faced discrimination. Others lived in small settlements on the outskirts, lacking resources and legal protection. The city's growth offered them few benefits, continuing the cycle of displacement begun under Spanish rule.

---

14. Boomtown Scams and Speculation

Real Estate Hype

As gold-related money circulated, some speculators started promoting **real estate** in and around Los Angeles. They published flyers exaggerating the fertility of the land or the closeness to major roads. Buyers, often from the eastern U.S., might invest in property unseen, hoping for quick profits. Some made money if the land was indeed valuable. Others discovered they had bought dry or remote plots.

Get-Rich-Quick Schemes

Various "gold-finding" machines or mining company stocks were sold to gullible folks passing through. Swindlers might salt worthless land with a few gold flakes to trick buyers. Some early "oil discoveries" were also faked to attract investors. While not as dramatic as in other frontier towns, Los Angeles saw its share of these scams, reflecting the desperate hopes of people seeking fortune.

15. Communication Advances

Telegraph Lines

The Gold Rush era sped up the **telegraph** system's spread in California. By the late 1850s and early 1860s, telegraph lines reached from Northern California to Southern California, including Los Angeles. This allowed messages to travel in hours instead of weeks. News of gold strikes, election results, or shipping schedules arrived faster. The telegraph also helped businesses coordinate supply deliveries, making the economy more efficient.

Newspapers Thrive

As literacy improved (though slowly), more newspapers popped up. Some targeted American readers with English articles on national events, gold prices, and city affairs. Others printed Spanish sections for Californios. News of strikes in the north or new immigration waves fueled ongoing interest in the gold economy. Editorials argued about city improvements, local politics, and the future direction of Los Angeles.

---

16. Influence on Agriculture

Vineyards and Orchards

Thanks to the new markets, Los Angeles vineyards expanded. Grapes found buyers among miners and city dwellers who wanted wine. Some farmers also planted fruit orchards—peaches, oranges, and pears—to supply the hungry goldfields. Transporting fresh fruit was tricky, so dried fruit or wine often proved more reliable. This laid an early foundation for Southern California's later fame as an agricultural hub.

Irrigation Innovations

With more profits from gold-related trade, some landowners invested in irrigation systems. They dug new ditches, built simple dams, or experimented with water wheels. While not advanced by modern standards, these projects increased the productivity of farmland. Over time, such innovations helped Los Angeles shift away from purely ranching to more diverse agriculture.

---

17. Cultural Mixing and Town Life

Cross-Cultural Marriages

The Gold Rush brought people of different backgrounds together. It was not uncommon for Americans to marry Californios or for European immigrants to marry into local families. These marriages helped bridge cultural gaps. Children from these unions often spoke both English and Spanish, playing a key role as interpreters. Over time, the city developed a unique identity that combined bits of Mexican, European, Asian, and American customs.

Entertainments and Celebrations

Public celebrations blended **fiesta** traditions with new American holidays like the Fourth of July. Parades included both Spanish guitars and brass bands. New foods appeared at festivals—tamales next to beef steaks, Chinese dumplings next to apple pies. This mix of traditions gave Los Angeles a festive reputation, even if serious social problems simmered beneath the surface.

18. Lasting Effects on the City's Growth

Strengthening Ties to the State

Although Northern California was the Gold Rush center, Los Angeles became more connected to Sacramento, San Francisco, and other regions through trade and travel routes. This pushed Los Angeles out of its old isolation. Politically, it gained representation in the state government, though it was often overshadowed by bigger cities in the north. Over time, these ties laid groundwork for future economic cooperation.

Shifts in Identity

Before the Gold Rush, Los Angeles was shaped by Spanish, Mexican, and early American influences. Afterward, it saw a blend of global cultures, a surge in commerce, and a slow move toward modern infrastructure. While many ranchos declined, new businesspeople and settlers took their place, forging a city that was no longer purely rural or purely Californio.

19. Challenges to Traditional Ways

Decline of Old Families

Many Californio families who once owned huge ranches found themselves squeezed by debts, lawsuits, and new competition. Some lost land to newcomers with cash from gold claims. Others adapted, investing in shops or smaller farms. A few managed to hold onto pieces of their heritage, but the era of large, unchallenged ranchos was fading fast.

Growing Inequality

The Gold Rush brought wealth to some, but not all. Laborers—Mexican, Chinese, or native—often faced low wages and poor living conditions. White Americans had easier access to land ownership and business loans, increasing the gap. Violence and unfair policies further hurt minority groups. This inequality would shape social tensions in Los Angeles for years to come.

CHAPTER 11

Railroads and the Changing Landscape

In the years following the Gold Rush, Los Angeles was still growing, but it lacked some of the connections that larger cities had. The roads were improving, and stagecoaches carried mail and passengers, but people wanted faster and more reliable transportation. Enter the **railroads**, which would transform Southern California in many ways. In this chapter, we will explore how railroads came to Los Angeles, who built them, and how they affected land use, population growth, and daily life. We will also see how these iron tracks linked Los Angeles to the rest of the country, pushing the city toward a bigger role in commerce and travel.

1. Early Plans for a Rail Connection

Dreams of a Railroad

Even before the Civil War (1861–1865), some local leaders in Los Angeles dreamed of a **railroad** that would connect the city to major markets. The city's remote location caused high shipping costs. Wagons and stagecoaches could only carry so much. The coastline lacked a good, deep-water port, and large ships had trouble docking at San Pedro. Merchants and farmers believed a railroad would solve many problems: it could move larger amounts of freight quickly, boost trade, and make travel simpler.

However, building a railroad was expensive. Investors needed confidence that enough freight and passengers would justify the cost. Also, the rough terrain between Los Angeles and other parts of California made construction difficult. There were deserts, mountains, and long distances with few towns in between. The population of the city was still small, meaning fewer local customers to support a rail line. Despite these concerns, planning discussions began.

Local Support and Hurdles

Some early efforts included local ranchers and businessmen teaming up. They formed committees or associations to raise funds. But money from Los Angeles alone was not enough. They needed support from larger companies or from the state or federal government. Additionally, some Californios whose families had lived here for generations were cautious. They worried the railroad would bring even more outsiders and speed up land sales, possibly displacing local people.

2. The Civil War and Its Aftermath

Wartime Delays

The **Civil War** in the eastern states (1861–1865) put many major projects on hold. The federal government focused on the war, and investors hesitated to spend money on big ventures. While a **transcontinental railroad** was underway farther north (eventually finished in 1869), linking Sacramento to the eastern states, Southern California had to wait. People in Los Angeles could see that railroads were the future, but for several years, progress was slow.

Post-War Renewals

When the war ended, the country turned its attention to expansion and rebuilding. Railroad companies, flush with new capital and encouraged by government land grants, began eyeing Southern California. They saw a chance to tap into ranching, farming, and the region's mild climate. Also, Los Angeles leaders saw that being connected to the transcontinental system might help them compete with San Francisco and other northern cities. By the late 1860s, talk of a **rail link** was stronger than ever.

3. The Los Angeles & San Pedro Railroad

A Local Line to the Coast

One of the first real breakthroughs for Los Angeles was a **short railroad** connecting the city to the harbor area near **San Pedro**. Completed in the late 1860s, this line was not very long—about 20 miles—but it made shipping goods much easier. Farmers or ranchers could load their products onto trains in downtown Los Angeles, and the train would carry them to the port. From there, smaller ships took the cargo to larger vessels waiting offshore.

This Los Angeles & San Pedro line was modest compared to big transcontinental routes. Still, it provided a powerful boost. The cost of moving freight dropped, and local agriculture could reach more markets. The city also used this line to receive building materials and consumer goods more quickly. Even though the harbor remained shallow, the rail connection saved time and money.

City Excitement Grows

Residents were thrilled. Newspapers ran headlines about the "modern age" arriving. They imagined future rail lines heading north, south, and east. Land prices rose near the new tracks because warehouses, factories, and businesses wanted to locate there. This short line demonstrated the potential benefits of better transportation, convincing more people to invest in larger rail projects.

---

4. The Southern Pacific and the First Link to the East

Powerhouse Railroad Companies

In the early 1870s, large railroad companies like the **Southern Pacific (SP)** began expanding. The Southern Pacific had connections to San Francisco and the Central Pacific (builders of part of the transcontinental railroad). Their executives believed that reaching Los Angeles would allow them to dominate rail traffic in California. By 1876, the Southern Pacific completed a line from northern California into Los Angeles through the **Newhall Pass** area. This was a huge step, finally linking Los Angeles by rail to the state's main rail network.

Driving the Golden Spike in Southern California

Though not as famous as the 1869 Golden Spike ceremony at Promontory Summit in Utah, the moment the SP line reached Los Angeles was still major news locally. The city threw celebrations. City leaders gave speeches about new prosperity. People lined up to watch the first trains roll in, carrying passengers and goods from the north. At last, Los Angeles could send oranges, wine, wool, and other products by rail to distant markets.

5. New Opportunities and Land Booms

Land Speculation

With the railroad in place, it became easier for people from San Francisco or the eastern states to visit and consider buying land. Real estate promoters launched **land booms**, advertising Los Angeles as a sunny paradise where crops flourished. Some folks bought property for farms, others for new towns. Prices shot up quickly, and some investors made fortunes by flipping land they had purchased cheaply a few years before.

Formation of New Towns

The 1870s and 1880s saw various **small towns** spring up along rail lines. Developers laid out streets, built hotels, and then advertised them in newspapers as health retreats or farming colonies. People from the Midwest or East Coast might read about "warm winters" and "profitable orange groves" and decide to hop on a train to start a new life. Not all these towns thrived, but many became part of the expanding Los Angeles region.

---

6. Problems and Setbacks

Drought and Financial Woes

The arrival of the railroad did not mean instant success for everyone. **Drought** still harmed crops, and some farmers could not repay loans taken to buy land at inflated prices. Additionally, rail construction was expensive. Railroad companies sometimes demanded **subsidies** from local governments, meaning cities or counties gave them land or money in return for routes. If the railroad did not bring enough revenue, both sides faced debt problems.

In the mid-1870s, there was also a national **economic downturn**. Banks failed, and many land speculators went bankrupt. This short depression slowed development in Los Angeles. Some building projects halted, and land prices fell. Still, the railroads kept running, and over time, the economy rebounded.

High Freight Costs and Monopolies

Because a few big companies, like the Southern Pacific, controlled most major lines in California, they could set **freight rates** as high as they wished. Farmers in Los Angeles complained that shipping oranges or grain cost too much, eating into their profits. There were political battles over "railroad monopolies," with newspapers calling the Southern Pacific the "Octopus" for its grip on state economics and politics. Yet farmers had limited choices, because without the rail, they had no fast way to ship goods to distant markets.

7. The Santa Fe Arrival and Rate Wars

A Rival Railroad Appears

For years, the Southern Pacific was the only major railroad serving Los Angeles. Then, in the 1880s, the **Atchison, Topeka and Santa Fe Railway** (often called the Santa Fe) decided to push into Southern California. Laying new tracks was costly, but the Santa Fe saw an opportunity to break SP's monopoly. In 1885, the Santa Fe line reached Los Angeles, creating competition for freight and passenger service.

The Great Rate War

To lure passengers and freight away from the Southern Pacific, the Santa Fe slashed ticket prices dramatically. At one point, a one-way ticket from the Midwest to Los Angeles dropped to just a few dollars. The Southern Pacific responded by lowering its prices, too. This **rate war** caused a surge of visitors to Los Angeles. Some were tourists, others were job seekers, and many were land buyers. Real estate activity soared again. Eventually, the railroads ended their fare war, but the damage and opportunities were done—thousands more people had arrived and stayed.

8. Changing City Life

Growth in Population

The new rail lines brought a steady stream of newcomers, both Americans from other states and immigrants from around the world. Los Angeles's population, which was once just a few thousand, climbed quickly. By the late 1880s, it reached over 50,000 residents. Though still smaller than San Francisco, Los Angeles was no longer just a dusty cattle town. Streets grew busy with pedestrians, wagons, and streetcars. More shops, hotels, and restaurants opened.

Modern Buildings and Services

With more people and money coming in, the city built **modern buildings** of brick and stone. Wooden structures remained, but downtown areas took on a more "urban" feel. Streetlights, often gas-powered (later replaced by electric lights), illuminated main roads. Horse-drawn streetcars carried passengers on rails set in city streets, making short-distance travel easier. People talked about paving roads, installing sewers, and creating public parks.

---

9. Impact on Agriculture

Better Shipping for Produce

Before railroads, farmers around Los Angeles could only sell large amounts of produce locally or ship it by slow wagon or boat. Now, they could load **citrus fruit**, grapes, and vegetables onto refrigerated railcars and send them across the country. This allowed them to reach big markets in the East, where fresh oranges from California were a novelty. The demand for Southern California produce grew, encouraging more farmers to plant orchards and vineyards.

Rise of Cooperative Marketing

As the railroad made large-scale shipping possible, farmers began forming **cooperatives**—groups that joined together to pack and market produce. By working together, they could negotiate better freight rates or build central packing houses by the tracks. This cooperative spirit would later become very important in the citrus industry, as we will see in the next chapter. But in these early days, it was enough to know that the railroad spurred farmers to organize more efficiently.

10. Land Development Companies

Boosters and Promotion

Entrepreneurs in Los Angeles realized that the railroad and pleasant climate could attract waves of settlers. They formed **land development companies** to buy large tracts of land, subdivide them, and sell smaller lots to newcomers. These boosters placed ads in eastern newspapers and sent pamphlets showing orange trees, palm-lined streets, and year-round sunshine. Many visitors arrived expecting a paradise. Some found success growing citrus or starting businesses. Others faced disappointment if they bought poor-quality land or lacked farming know-how.

Planned Suburbs

Along the rail lines radiating from downtown, new "suburban" areas sprouted. Developers built neat grids of streets and advertised them as ideal neighborhoods for families seeking clean air away from busy downtown. People could ride the train into the city for work or shopping, then return to their quiet home in the evening. While some suburbs remained farmland for years, others quickly filled with homes, schools, and churches.

11. Social and Cultural Shifts

Changing Demographics

With the railroad bringing more people from different backgrounds, Los Angeles became more diverse. The city's old Californio families, newcomers from the eastern U.S., European immigrants, and a growing Chinese community all lived side by side. Conflicts arose over language, religion, and customs, but many people learned to cooperate for business or community projects. Bilingual signs still appeared in some neighborhoods, while English-only schools grew more common.

Leisure and Tourism

The new lines also made it easier for **tourists** to visit the beaches and warm inland valleys. Visitors came in winter to escape cold climates back east. Small seaside towns like Santa Monica or Long Beach benefited from short rail spurs that carried day-trippers seeking sun and ocean views. Hotels sprang up to serve these seasonal guests. Tourism became a small but growing part of the economy, hinting at a bigger trend that would later define the region.

---

12. Labor on the Rails

Construction and Maintenance

Building railroads required intense labor. Companies hired large crews to lay tracks, dig tunnels, and construct bridges. Many laborers were **Chinese immigrants**, who had also worked on the transcontinental railroad in the north. They faced low pay and tough working conditions, blasting through rock or laying ties in scorching desert heat. Other groups, such as Mexican laborers or workers from Europe, also joined. After the tracks were built, maintenance crews had to keep them in good shape, removing debris from desert winds or repairing damage from flash floods.

Workers' Living Conditions

Railroad workers often lived in temporary camps near construction sites. They slept in tents or simple barracks, far from the comforts of city life.

Food might be basic, like beans, rice, and salted meat. Illness spread easily, and medical care was limited. Although the railroads transformed Los Angeles, the laborers who built them seldom shared in the large profits. They did important, dangerous work but remained at the lower end of the economic ladder.

13. Political Influence of Railroads

Power in Sacramento and Washington

Railroad executives, especially those from the Southern Pacific, wielded great **political power**. They lobbied (or bribed) lawmakers to pass friendly legislation, grant land, or allow them to set high freight rates. Newspapers often criticized the railroads for having too much influence, calling their top officials "railroad barons." Protests and public meetings pressed for regulation, but success came slowly. Over time, California did pass some laws to control rail monopolies, though rail companies continued to push back.

Local Politics and Development

In Los Angeles, city councils and county boards vied to attract new rail lines or extend existing ones. They might offer tax breaks or free rights-of-way to railroad companies. Some officials gained popularity by promising more rail connections, which could boost property values and create jobs. Others worried about potential debt or corruption. Still, most residents agreed that without railroads, Los Angeles would lag behind.

14. Environmental Changes

Remaking the Land

Railroads encouraged more farmland development, leading to more irrigation ditches, wells, and eventually greater demands for water.

Hillsides might be cleared to make way for tracks or farmland. Wildlife habitats shrank. While people enjoyed the benefits of modern transport, the region's natural balance changed. Native plants, which thrived on scarce rainfall, gave way to fields of wheat or orchards needing heavy watering.

Floods and Washouts

Southern California's rivers could flood fiercely after heavy rains. Rail lines built near riverbanks sometimes got washed out. Crews had to rebuild tracks or construct taller bridges. Companies began to straighten river channels or pile rocks along banks to protect their investment. This caused new shifts in how water flowed, sometimes increasing flood risk downstream. Early railroad maps show how lines had to bend around canyons and cross rivers on wooden trestles, which were vulnerable in storm seasons.

---

15. Rivalries and Cooperation

City vs. City

As the railroad network spread, different towns competed to become the main stop. For example, San Bernardino, Riverside, and others wanted rail stations to attract settlers and businesses. Sometimes a railroad company bypassed a town whose leaders refused to give enough incentives. This could make the difference between a community thriving or remaining small. Los Angeles had to keep promoting itself so railroads would favor it over San Diego or other ports.

Building Branch Lines

Cooperation also grew. Farmers in distant valleys wanted a branch line so they could ship their goods to Los Angeles or beyond. Local groups pooled money or convinced county officials to fund these "feeder lines." Soon, spidery tracks spread through the region. Although each branch line added cost to the railroad company, it also opened up more farmland, which created more business. This cycle fed Los Angeles' rise as a central hub.

16. Daily Travel and Commuting

Passenger Service

Not all trains carried freight. Passenger trains soon offered daily service between Los Angeles and nearby towns like Pasadena, Anaheim, or San Bernardino. People could visit friends, attend church, or do business without spending hours on dusty roads. Even short trips felt luxurious compared to wagon travel. Train schedules were printed in newspapers, and families planned outings around them.

Early Commuters

Some folks who worked in the city chose to live outside it, riding the train in the morning and returning at night. This was the start of the **commuter** idea, which would grow larger in later decades. At first, only a few well-off individuals did this, because tickets could be expensive. Over time, more services appeared, including discounted fares for regular riders. This commuting pattern helped shape the spread of neighborhoods around Los Angeles.

---

17. Boosting Local Industries

Wine and Oil

We have seen how citrus farming benefited from railroads, but other industries also grew. **Wine producers** around Los Angeles shipped barrels across the region, giving California wine more recognition. Early **oil wells** were drilled in places like Pico Canyon (north of Los Angeles) in the 1870s, and once oil was extracted, trains carried it to markets. This foreshadowed an even bigger oil boom in the 20th century.

Manufacturing and Trade

Some factories producing goods like soap, canned fruit, or machinery found it easier to locate in Los Angeles, where they had rail access. This spurred the birth of a **manufacturing sector**. While the city was not as industrialized as parts of the East Coast, it no longer relied solely on agriculture. A handful of **wholesale** trade houses also set up near rail yards, distributing goods throughout Southern California.

18. The 1880s Boom and Bust

Wild Speculation

The mid-1880s, especially after the Santa Fe arrived, brought an extraordinary **land boom**. Real estate prices soared, sometimes doubling or tripling in months. Buyers from across the country swarmed in, hoping to profit from the sunny climate and new railroad connections. Townsites were laid out overnight, and fancy brochures promised fortunes to anyone who bought land.

Collapse of the Boom

Like many booms built on speculation, this one could not last. By the late 1880s, prices crashed. Many people who bought expensive lots could not sell them at a profit. Banks failed, and some developers went bankrupt. While the city's population had jumped during the boom, the aftermath left empty subdivisions, half-finished buildings, and financial pain for many. Still, the rail network remained, and enough new residents stayed to keep Los Angeles growing, just at a slower pace.

19. Shaping Los Angeles Identity

A Railroad Town Evolving

By the end of the 1880s, Los Angeles was no longer a hidden corner of California. Trains ran regularly, linking it with other parts of the state and with the rest of the country. It was building a reputation for **mild weather**, **healthy living**, and **agricultural opportunities**. Newspapers in Chicago or New York wrote stories about "Los Angeles: The Future Metropolis of the West," praising the rail lines that made it reachable.

Seeds for the Future

While we will learn more in later chapters about water projects, oil booms, and Hollywood, it was the **railroads** that first set Los Angeles on the path to a broader economy. They allowed more than local trade; they encouraged large-scale migration, big farming, and a sense of connection to the nation. Problems with monopolies, high freight rates, and land speculation did not vanish, but the city had taken a big step toward modernity.

---

20. Chapter Summary

With the railroad era in full swing, Los Angeles had taken a great leap forward. People could imagine an even brighter future if they could harness the region's mild weather and soil for **agriculture**. That is exactly what we will explore in the next chapter: the growth of **citrus farming** and other crops, and how this helped Los Angeles shift from a frontier town to a bustling agricultural center that fed markets across the country.

CHAPTER 12

The Rise of Agriculture and Citrus

By the late 1800s, the rails were bringing more people and goods into Los Angeles. At the same time, the region's warm climate and improved irrigation methods helped farmers expand their fields and orchards. In this chapter, we will look at how agriculture—especially **citrus farming**—became a major force in Southern California's economy. We will see how local growers formed groups to market their produce, how new irrigation techniques changed the land, and how this wave of farming shaped the city's character before the arrival of more modern times.

1. Early Farming Roots

Grain and Grapes

Before citrus orchards dominated the landscape, Los Angeles farmers grew many crops. Wheat, barley, and corn were common after the ranchos began to break up. Some smaller fields yielded **vegetables** for local markets, while vineyards produced grapes for wine. In fact, wine was quite important in early Los Angeles, with dozens of small wineries operating near the river or in surrounding valleys. However, shipping wine long distances was tricky, and local demand was not huge.

The Limits of Local Sales

Without railroads, farmers in the 1860s could only sell large amounts of produce if they lived close to the city, or if they risked shipping by wagon to the harbor at San Pedro. When the railroad arrived, this changed. Farmers now realized they could grow crops to send across the state or even to other parts of the country, assuming they could keep the produce fresh. This possibility opened the door to more varied and profitable agriculture.

2. Early Citrus Experiments

The First Orange Trees

Citrus trees—especially **orange** trees—came to California with the Spanish missions, which grew them for local use. By the mid-1800s, some Californios and American settlers had small family orchards. They discovered that the sunny climate and mild winters made this region ideal for citrus. Rainfall was not high, but with irrigation ditches, trees thrived. Oranges, lemons, and limes found a happy home in Southern California soil.

However, selling these fruits was not easy at first. Fresh oranges could spoil on a long wagon journey, and local demand was limited. Most families who planted orange trees did so for personal use or small-scale sales in town.

A Taste for Oranges

Visitors from cold regions, like the Midwest or East Coast, were thrilled to see "golden oranges" growing in winter. They spread the word that California oranges were sweet and full of juice. This interest turned into real business potential once the railroads began running. If farmers could get their oranges to distant cities quickly, they could sell them at good prices when snow covered farms in other states.

---

3. The Role of Railroads in Farming Success

Faster Transport of Fresh Produce

As we saw in the last chapter, the **railroads** gave Los Angeles farmers a huge advantage. A train with **refrigerated cars** (cooled by ice) could carry oranges or other perishable items to places like Chicago or St. Louis within days. This meant East Coast customers could enjoy fresh oranges long before local orchards there blossomed. Demand soared for California citrus.

New Markets and Higher Prices

Because oranges were rare in winter in much of the country, consumers paid premium prices. Southern California growers discovered they could make good profits if they managed their orchards well, avoided pests, and timed harvests to meet market demand. Over time, more local land switched from grain or ranching to orange groves and lemon groves, changing the region's agricultural identity.

---

4. Irrigation and Water Innovations

Water Scarcity

Southern California's climate is semi-arid, meaning it has mild winters and hot, dry summers with limited rainfall. Growing citrus or other thirsty crops required irrigation. Early on, farmers relied on **zanjas** (ditches) that diverted water from the Los Angeles River or smaller streams. But as more orchards emerged, water supplies began to strain. Conflicts arose among farmers over water rights, especially in years of low rainfall.

Irrigation Districts

To solve these problems, groups of farmers formed **irrigation districts**. In these districts, landowners joined forces to build canals, dams, or storage ponds. They pooled money to dig deeper ditches or even drill wells. Laws passed by the state allowed them to tax themselves to fund these projects. The result was more stable water delivery, though not always perfect. In some areas, private water companies formed, charging farmers for the amount of water used.

Technological Improvements

Meanwhile, new **pumping technology** emerged, letting farmers draw water from underground aquifers. Windmills or early gas-powered pumps became common sights in orchard areas. Engineers experimented with clay pipes or steel pipes to move water over longer distances. All these changes meant citrus orchards could spread beyond the immediate reach of the Los Angeles River.

5. Formation of Citrus Colonies

Organized Settlements

Land developers saw that citrus farming was profitable. They began creating "citrus colonies," planned communities focused on orchards. They advertised these colonies in eastern newspapers, promising a ready-made farm and home. Buyers would get a plot of land with young orange or lemon trees already planted, plus a share in the local irrigation system. This appealed to retired soldiers, teachers, or city workers looking for a healthier lifestyle.

Notable Citrus Communities

Towns like **Riverside**, **Redlands**, and **Orange** (though a bit farther from the city) were prime examples of these citrus-based communities. Closer to Los Angeles, places like **Pasadena** also showcased orange groves in the nearby foothills. These areas boasted scenic views and cooler nights, which some said produced sweeter oranges. New residents, often from the Midwest, tried their hand at orchard management, learning about pruning, pest control, and packing fruit for shipment.

---

6. The Birth of Cooperative Marketing

The Citrus "Brand"

Even though citrus farmers could ship their fruit by rail, they faced competition from each other and from other states, such as Florida. How would a grocer in Chicago decide which oranges to buy? If each farmer acted alone, prices might drop too low. The solution was **cooperative marketing**: farmers banded together to pack fruit in a common brand, guaranteeing consistent quality.

In the late 1880s and early 1890s, local grower associations formed, agreeing on standards for picking and packing. They might share a single label or trademark to build customer trust. This set the stage for famous brands that would emerge in the early 20th century. At this point, the idea was that cooperation improved profits, stabilized prices, and kept quality high.

Early Packing Houses

These associations built **packing houses** near rail lines, where workers sorted oranges by size and quality. They packed them in wooden crates with brightly printed labels showing sunny groves or appealing logos. This branding helped stores recognize California citrus. Farmers learned that a neat, uniform crate could attract better prices than mismatched or poorly handled fruit.

---

7. Labor on the Orchards

Who Worked the Fields?

Cultivating large orchards required steady labor. **Mexican workers**, many of whom had lived in the region for generations or came from across the border, formed a major part of the workforce. Some native people also did field tasks. Over time, other groups, including immigrants from Asia and Europe, joined. Wages were not high, and workers often faced rough conditions: hot sun, long hours, and limited housing. Yet orchard work was steady compared to seasonal harvests for other crops.

Living Conditions and Challenges

Farm laborers might live in camps set up by farm owners or in small houses near the orchards. Conditions varied: some camps had basic facilities, while others lacked clean water or proper sanitation. Workers had few legal protections, meaning long hours with few breaks. Despite these challenges, the lure of consistent work in the orchard areas attracted people from rural parts of Mexico or other parts of California who needed jobs.

---

8. Growth Beyond Oranges

Lemons, Grapefruits, and More

While oranges led the citrus boom, other fruits also gained attention. **Lemons** did well in coastal areas where the climate was slightly cooler.

Grapefruits, which needed warmth and space, appeared in some inland valleys. Farmers also tried olives, apricots, peaches, and walnuts. The advantage of citrus, however, was that the fruit could survive shipping better, especially if picked at the right time and protected in crates.

Vegetable and Flower Farms

Not every grower went into citrus. Some found success with **vegetables** like celery, beans, or peppers, selling them to the growing city population or shipping them out by rail. Flowers also became a niche business, with certain areas specializing in growing blooms for bouquets and decorative arrangements. This variety enriched the region's agriculture, though citrus remained the star.

---

9. The Booms and Busts in Farming

Overplanting and Market Gluts

As word spread that citrus farming was profitable, more people jumped in. Land speculators carved up big ranches into orchard lots, selling them to hopeful newcomers. Sometimes, this led to **overplanting**: too many orange groves, producing more fruit than the market could handle. Prices could tumble, leaving farmers stuck with low incomes. Some orchardists lost money or had to switch to different crops.

Diseases and Pests

Orange trees faced threats like **scale insects**, **fungus**, and other pests. Without modern pesticides, farmers tried various remedies, from smearing trees with oils to using ladybugs (a natural predator for some pests). A bad infestation could ruin a crop or kill trees, setting a farmer back years. Over time, agricultural experiment stations offered advice on pest control, and growers began to share strategies through cooperatives.

10. City and Agriculture Intertwine

Los Angeles as an Agricultural Hub

Despite occasional setbacks, by the late 1880s and early 1890s, Los Angeles was recognized as a center for **citrus shipping**. Railroads built special icing stations to keep fruit cold on long journeys. The city had numerous packing houses, and local banks loaned money to orchard owners. Real estate near fertile areas soared in price, especially if it included water rights.

Rise of a "Citrus Culture"

Many city dwellers enjoyed seeing rows of orange or lemon trees on the horizon. It gave the region a special charm. Advertisements boasted of a place where you could pick fresh oranges on Christmas Day. Tourism promoters showed pictures of healthy orchard workers under clear blue skies, luring more settlers. This image of an **orange paradise** stuck in people's minds, shaping how Los Angeles was viewed nationwide.

11. Marketing the Sunshine

Health and Climate Advertising

One reason citrus thrived was because of **marketing** that tied fruit to health and the Southern California climate. Orange juice was promoted as a cure for colds or a source of vitamins (even before modern science confirmed vitamin C's benefits). Land developers promised that living among the orange groves would be good for people's lungs, especially those from colder, damp climates.

Tourist Attraction

Orchards themselves became a tourist draw. Some orchard owners let visitors walk among the trees or sample fresh fruit. Photographs of blossoming orange trees with snow-capped mountains in the distance were used in brochures to show the region's unique blend of mild weather and dramatic scenery. This publicity made more people from across the country want to experience Los Angeles firsthand.

---

12. Community Growth and Infrastructure

Small Towns Around Orchards

As citrus expanded, small farm towns near Los Angeles added schools, churches, and stores. Many were laid out with a central plaza or main street, reflecting older Spanish traditions or modern American planning. The local train station was often the heart of the town, sending out crates of fruit and receiving new settlers. Over time, some of these orchard towns merged into the larger Los Angeles metropolitan area.

Roads and Bridges

Though rail was essential for long-distance shipping, local roads were needed to bring fruit from orchards to packing houses or rail depots. So counties built or improved roads, including wooden or steel bridges over creeks. Horse-drawn wagons carried crates to shipping points, and in some places, trolley lines or narrow-gauge railways connected orchard regions to the city. These improvements also encouraged other businesses, like hardware stores and blacksmith shops, to open in rural areas.

13. Conflicts Over Land and Water

Disputes with Ranching

As farmland replaced cattle ranches, tensions arose. Some ranchers held out, wanting open range for their herds. They might resent orchardists who fenced off fields or diverted water for irrigation. In turn, orchard owners disliked free-roaming cattle trampling young trees or muddying irrigation ditches. Local governments had to pass **fencing laws** and set rules for livestock to resolve these conflicts.

Farmers vs. City Growth

As Los Angeles expanded, farmland near the city limits became attractive for housing or commercial development. **Real estate speculators** approached orchard owners, offering high prices for their land. Some farmers sold out, making big profits but reducing the total orchard acreage. This tension between urban expansion and farmland preservation would keep growing in the years to come.

14. Labor Movements and Social Issues

Worker Organizations

Though not as large as in heavy industry, farm laborers and packing house workers sometimes tried to organize for better wages or conditions. A few **labor unions** emerged, but orchard owners were often resistant, fearing higher costs. Disputes led to strikes or lockouts, but these did not become widespread. The flow of new immigrants looking for work made it hard for labor groups to build unity.

Housing and Segregation

Many farmworkers were of Mexican heritage, and they often lived in separate neighborhoods or labor camps. Some orchard towns quietly practiced **segregation** in schools or housing. This meant workers' children received fewer educational resources, and living conditions were often poor. While some orchard owners treated their workers decently, the general system favored landowners, leaving laborers with little power to demand improvements.

---

15. The Broader Impact on Los Angeles

Economic Boost

The success of citrus and other agriculture gave Los Angeles a **steady economic base** beyond ranching and speculation. Money from citrus sales flowed into local banks, which financed new businesses. Railroads profited from shipping fees, and packing houses employed hundreds of workers. By the late 1890s, agriculture was a pillar of the regional economy, helping Los Angeles ride out future economic ups and downs.

Cultural Celebrations

Communities began to hold **citrus festivals** or harvest fairs. Parades featured floats decorated with oranges and lemons. These events became annual traditions, bringing townspeople together to celebrate a successful harvest. Visitors from the city or other states marveled at the displays, further linking agriculture with community pride.

---

16. Threats to Orchards

Winter Freezes

While generally mild, Southern California did occasionally suffer **cold snaps** that could damage fruit. A sudden frost could kill blossoms or make oranges drop prematurely. Farmers began using small smudge pots that burned oil to produce heat around trees on cold nights. This process saved many crops, but it required vigilance and extra labor.

Competition from Other Regions

As the citrus industry succeeded in Southern California, growers in other states, like Florida or Arizona, also expanded. If their fruit reached markets at the same time, prices could fall. Overproduction in California itself was also a risk, so cooperative marketing became even more important to avoid glutted markets.

17. Early Science and Education in Farming

Agricultural Experiment Stations

The state of California and some local colleges set up **experiment stations** to study citrus cultivation, pest control, and soil management. Scientists tested new irrigation methods or fertilizers, sharing discoveries with farmers. This helped orchards remain competitive and healthy. It also sparked the idea that farming could benefit from formal research, not just tradition or guesswork.

Teaching Future Farmers

As more schools opened in rural areas, some offered basic agricultural classes. Students learned about pruning, grafting, and orchard management. Local 4-H clubs or farming groups gave young people hands-on practice. This emphasis on **practical agriculture** supported a new generation that viewed farming as a modern, scientific pursuit, not a backward chore.

18. Los Angeles on the Eve of a New Century

Diversifying Economy

By the late 1890s, Los Angeles was no longer a one-industry town. Agriculture, boosted by citrus, was strong. The city also had some manufacturing, oil exploration, tourism, and real estate development. This **diverse economy** made the region more resilient to single-crop failures. Yet agriculture remained central to its identity, symbolized by those endless rows of orange trees.

Urban and Rural Mix

Visitors to Los Angeles around 1900 saw a curious mix: a growing downtown with modern buildings and bustling streets, and, just beyond, orchards stretching for miles. Streetcars carried city dwellers past fruit groves, reminding everyone how close farmland was to urban life. This blend of agriculture and city culture set Los Angeles apart from many eastern industrial centers.

---

19. A Lasting Legacy

National Recognition

Citrus from Southern California gained a reputation for quality. Advertisements called them "The Finest Oranges in the World" or "Nature's Perfect Fruit." Grocery stores across America carried crates stamped with names of Los Angeles-area growers. This boosted the region's fame, encouraging even more visitors and settlers to see where these delicious oranges came from.

Foundation for Future Growth

The farming boom laid groundwork for bigger developments in the early 20th century. Profits from oranges funded infrastructure, including roads, schools, and civic buildings. As new technologies emerged—like better refrigeration, electric power, and automobiles—Los Angeles would be ready to adapt and push forward. The success of cooperative marketing paved the way for larger groups (like Sunkist in the early 1900s) that would make Southern California citrus a household name.

CHAPTER 13

Early 20th Century: Shaping a New City

By the dawn of the 1900s, Los Angeles had grown from a sleepy agricultural settlement into a bustling city with rail connections and thriving orchards. Yet it was still on the edge of something bigger. In this chapter, we will look at how Los Angeles evolved in the early 20th century, focusing on the period from around 1900 to the mid-1920s. We will see new forms of transportation, shifting neighborhoods, and the rise of industries that would soon redefine the city. While we will not jump too far into modern times, we will show how this era set the stage for many later developments.

1. Setting the Stage at the Turn of the Century

Population Growth

At the start of the 1900s, Los Angeles' population had already surged thanks to the railroads and the citrus boom. The city reached about 100,000 residents by 1900—a big jump from just a few decades earlier. Streets downtown were busy with horse-drawn carriages, wagons delivering farm produce, and electric streetcars carrying passengers. Buildings with two or three stories were common, and a few taller structures (five or six stories) hinted at future skyscrapers.

Some areas still held farmland, but neighborhoods were spreading outward. This growth brought challenges: how would the city provide services like paved roads, clean water, and reliable electricity to so many new people? City leaders and boosters argued that Los Angeles needed to keep improving infrastructure to sustain its ambition of becoming a major urban center on the West Coast.

Continuation of the Railroad Influence

Railroads, such as the Southern Pacific and Santa Fe, still played a huge role in shipping goods and bringing in new arrivals. Trains transported citrus, vegetables, oil, and manufactured items from local factories. People who read about the "land of sunshine" decided to move here, hoping to start businesses or enjoy a healthier life in the mild climate. Meanwhile, competition between rail lines kept freight rates somewhat in check, which encouraged further growth.

2. The Electric Streetcar Revolution

The Birth of the Pacific Electric

One of the most important developments in early 20th-century Los Angeles was the spread of **electric streetcars**. Although some streetcar lines existed before 1900, they became a major force under business leaders like **Henry E. Huntington**, who created the **Pacific Electric Railway** in 1901. This system—often called the "Red Cars"—spread across Los Angeles and its surrounding regions, connecting downtown to places like Pasadena, Long Beach, Santa Monica, and dozens of smaller towns.

These electric streetcars were faster and cleaner than horse-drawn trolleys. They used overhead electric wires, allowing them to glide along tracks without producing the smoke and noise of steam engines. The Pacific Electric system eventually became one of the largest interurban networks in the world, with hundreds of miles of track and bright red cars carrying thousands of passengers daily.

Impact on Neighborhoods

Because the streetcars made travel easier, people could live farther from the city center. Suburbs sprang up around streetcar stops. A worker in downtown Los Angeles might buy a home in Pasadena and ride the Red Car to the office each morning. This pattern reshaped the region, creating many "streetcar suburbs" with single-family homes, small commercial strips, and local schools. Over time, farmland gave way to residential blocks, and small towns like Glendale or Alhambra grew into bustling communities.

3. Changing City Government and Services

The Role of City Hall

With rapid population growth, local government had to keep up. The **Los Angeles City Council** debated how to pave streets, lay sewer lines, and ensure enough police officers patrolled the expanding neighborhoods. Taxes rose as leaders pushed for bigger projects, such as road paving or the construction of public buildings. Voters elected mayors and council members who promised modern improvements—streetlights, libraries, and expanded fire departments.

In many cases, these leaders worked closely with real estate developers and railroad owners, hoping that public projects would attract more residents and investors. Some critics argued that wealthier interests had too much sway in City Hall, shaping policies to benefit their own land deals. Still, most Angelenos agreed that the city needed to invest in infrastructure to become a true metropolis.

Public Health and Sanitation

As Los Angeles grew, so did concerns about cleanliness and disease. Open sewers and unpaved streets caused foul smells and unsanitary conditions. Local doctors worried about epidemics like typhoid or tuberculosis. In response, the city gradually improved garbage collection and built better sewer systems. Health inspectors tried to ensure that dairies, meatpacking houses, and canneries followed basic hygiene rules. While these efforts were not perfect, they helped reduce the worst health risks of an overcrowded town.

---

4. The Growing Presence of Automobiles

Early Cars Appear

Although horses, wagons, and streetcars still dominated Los Angeles traffic in 1900, the **automobile** was on the horizon. The first cars were expensive, noisy, and sometimes unreliable. Wealthy enthusiasts imported them or bought early models from local inventors. Neighbors often gawked at these "horseless carriages," which could scare horses and cause confusion on dusty roads.

Within a decade, cars improved, and more middle-class families considered buying them. Los Angeles, with its spread-out layout and mild weather, seemed perfect for automobiles. Even though this was not yet a "car city," the seeds were planted. Roads soon needed to be widened or paved with better materials to accommodate faster car travel. Gasoline stations appeared in small numbers, and mechanics opened shops to fix these new machines.

Boosters and Motor Tourism

Early 20th-century boosters realized that cars might draw tourists. Pamphlets encouraged people to drive to scenic spots, praising the region's good roads (although many were still rough) and year-round driving weather. Adventurous tourists from other states sometimes embarked on long cross-country journeys to see Southern California, though such trips were challenging before national highways. This early wave of "motor tourism" would expand in later decades, but the foundation was already visible.

5. Oil Discoveries and Industrial Growth

Oil Wells in the City

Los Angeles had known small oil fields since the 1870s, but the early 1900s brought bigger discoveries. Wells sprang up in neighborhoods like **Echo Park** and further south, tapping into rich petroleum reserves beneath the city. For many residents, it was odd to see oil derricks towering behind houses or near beaches. While these wells provided jobs and boosted the economy, they also caused noise, pollution, and occasional spills.

Over time, more large fields were found, and Los Angeles became a center of **oil production**. Companies like Union Oil and Standard Oil established offices and refineries. The wealth generated from oil spurred real estate deals, bank expansions, and city improvements. Yet concerns grew about the environmental effects and potential fires or accidents in densely populated areas.

Factories and Manufacturing

Though agriculture still thrived, the city also gained more **factories** producing goods like rubber tires, metal parts, chemicals, or canned foods. Some entrepreneurs saw Los Angeles as a strategic location—close to harbors, rail lines, and farmland. The local workforce, including many recent immigrants, provided labor. As new industries formed, the economy diversified. People no longer had to rely only on oranges, tourism, and land speculation.

---

6. Cultural Shifts in a Growing Metropolis

Immigrant Communities

Los Angeles in the early 1900s drew newcomers from around the world. Mexican migration increased, partly due to the Mexican Revolution (1910–1920), which displaced many families. Chinese and Japanese immigrants, despite facing discrimination, continued to form vibrant communities with their own shops, temples, and social clubs. European immigrants from Italy, Germany, and other countries also arrived, seeking jobs in factories or the booming construction trade.

These groups added new foods, languages, and traditions to the city. Neighborhoods like **Chinatown** or **Little Tokyo** took shape near downtown. African American families also began moving from the South, finding work in railroads, agriculture, or domestic service. While they encountered prejudice, they built churches, businesses, and social organizations that strengthened their communities. Diversity became a hallmark of the city, though tensions over housing and jobs simmered beneath the surface.

Arts and Leisure

A growing population wanted more than just work; they wanted entertainment. Early theaters showed **vaudeville acts**—live variety shows with comedy, music, and dancing. Cinemas were just beginning to appear, screening silent movies. Public parks, like **Elysian Park** or those near the downtown, offered green space for picnics. Beach communities—such as Santa Monica or Venice—became leisure spots, with piers featuring arcades, merry-go-rounds, and fun rides.

Churches and civic groups organized festivals and parades. The city's multi-ethnic makeup meant there were events celebrating Mexican Independence Day, Chinese New Year, and various European holidays. This lively mix of cultural celebrations gave Los Angeles a festive atmosphere, even as city dwellers worked hard to make ends meet.

---

7. Annexations and City Expansion

Swallowing Neighboring Towns

As Los Angeles leaders aimed to create a larger, more powerful city, they looked to absorb nearby communities. Smaller towns agreed to **annexation** if Los Angeles promised better water systems, police protection, or street paving. By the early 1910s, places like **Highland Park**, **Hollywood**, and **Watts** joined the city. This annexation strategy allowed Los Angeles to expand its tax base and territory, strengthening its position in the region.

Sometimes these mergers caused friction. Local leaders worried they would lose control over local affairs. Residents feared higher taxes or different rules. Yet many were persuaded by the promise of city services. Over time, Los Angeles' boundaries stretched from the downtown core to the Pacific Ocean and encompassed vast suburban tracts—laying the groundwork for a sprawling metropolis.

The Hollywood Annexation

Hollywood was one of the most famous annexations, occurring in 1910. At that time, Hollywood was a small independent city with its own identity.

But water shortages and limited services pushed Hollywood's leaders to join Los Angeles, which had a larger water system and more money for infrastructure. Though Hollywood was not yet the global film capital, a few movie studios had begun operations there. Annexation ensured it would grow under Los Angeles' umbrella.

8. Education and Early Colleges

Public School Growth

With more families arriving, the **Los Angeles Unified School District** expanded rapidly. New elementary and high schools were built in suburban areas, each trying to keep class sizes manageable. Early schools often had strict rules—students learned reading, writing, arithmetic, and basic history. Separate schools existed for certain minority communities, reflecting broader segregation policies of the era. Still, the city's emphasis on building schools signaled that education was becoming a public priority.

Emerging Colleges and Universities

A few colleges also began to gain footing. The **University of Southern California (USC)**, founded in 1880, grew steadily. The **University of California** opened a branch in Los Angeles later on (1919), though it took time to become a full-fledged campus. Other private institutions started smaller programs, often focusing on teacher training or religious studies. By the 1920s, the idea that Los Angeles could be an academic center gained momentum, but it was still in early stages compared to older universities in Northern California or the East Coast.

9. Boosters and Civic Pride

The Role of Boosters

Much of Los Angeles' development in this era can be traced to **civic boosters**—enthusiastic promoters who published brochures, wrote newspaper articles, and staged events to praise the city's potential. Figures like **Harrison Gray Otis** (owner of the Los Angeles Times) and **Harry Chandler** used their platforms to attract new settlers, business leaders, and investors. They touted the city's sunshine, farmland, and "unlimited" resources, sometimes glossing over problems like water scarcity or poverty.

These boosters strongly believed that the city's future was bright if it continued to expand. They organized exhibitions, traveled to other states to speak about opportunities here, and sent out thousands of postcards showing orange groves and palm trees. While critics said they exaggerated, the booster message worked, luring thousands of people each year.

Civic Associations

Groups like the **Chamber of Commerce** and the **Merchants and Manufacturers Association** coordinated business events and lobbied local government. They worked on city beautification projects, planting palm trees along major streets to give Los Angeles a distinctive look. They pushed for modern street lighting and tidy parks, hoping to make a positive impression on tourists. The city's shift from a dusty frontier outpost to a polished urban center was partly guided by these organized efforts.

10. Challenges of Labor and Race Relations

Labor Disputes

Industrial growth in oil, factories, and shipping led to the rise of **labor unions**. Workers sought better wages and conditions. Employers often resisted union demands. Clashes sometimes turned violent, with strikes or lockouts. Police and private security forces broke up protests, leading to arrests or injuries. Although Los Angeles never became as strongly unionized as some eastern cities, these early struggles set the tone for future labor issues.

Racial Tensions

Los Angeles' diverse population faced ongoing discrimination. African Americans had difficulty buying homes outside certain areas. Asian immigrants encountered laws limiting property ownership. Mexican workers often lived in overcrowded neighborhoods near factories or agricultural fields. Occasional riots or racial violence made headlines, revealing deep social divides. While the city prided itself on being welcoming, the reality was more complicated, with prejudice affecting housing, jobs, and public services.

11. The Women's Suffrage Movement

Women's Clubs and Activists

Women in Los Angeles formed clubs to discuss education, public health, and social reform. These groups played a big part in the **women's suffrage movement**—the drive to gain the right to vote. Activists like **Caroline Severance** and others hosted meetings, wrote letters, and held rallies. By 1911, California gave women the right to vote in state elections, years before the federal amendment passed (1920).

Impact on City Politics

With women voting and running for local office, the political landscape changed. Women often pushed for better schools, parks, and child welfare programs. They also fought against corruption in city government. While progress was slow, Los Angeles became an example of how women's participation in politics could reshape local policies. This shift was part of a broader national movement toward recognizing women's voices in public affairs.

12. The Rise of Motion Pictures

Early Film Studios

In the 1900s, a few **film studios** moved from the East Coast to the Los Angeles area, drawn by sunny weather that allowed outdoor filming nearly all year. Small production companies set up makeshift stages in Hollywood or downtown. Directors discovered they could find desert, beach, and mountain locations within an easy drive. By 1910, movie-making was a growing local industry, though not yet the massive enterprise it would become.

Effects on Local Life

Film crews wandering around neighborhoods or farmland amused local residents. Some saw it as a novelty, while others noticed that these studios hired carpenters, seamstresses, and actors, boosting the economy. As the film business expanded, outsiders labeled Los Angeles a budding movie town. Even though the city was still known more for agriculture and commerce, the seeds of the future Hollywood identity were sown here in these early decades.

---

13. Conservation and Parks

Calls to Preserve Nature

The rapid spread of housing and industry worried some residents who loved the natural beauty of Southern California. Local officials and civic groups began discussing **parklands** and the need to conserve open spaces. Places like **Griffith Park** were donated or purchased to protect hillsides from development. City planners debated how to balance growth with green areas for recreation.

Hetch Hetchy Influence and Local Efforts

Although Hetch Hetchy Valley is in Northern California, its damming (to provide San Francisco with water) sparked a wider conservation debate. In Los Angeles, a few voices questioned whether the region should keep building outward or pay more attention to preserving rivers, wetlands, and forests. Still, city boosters mostly favored expansion. Conservation efforts remained relatively small during this period, though they laid a foundation for future environmental movements.

14. Social Life and Entertainment

Music and Theater

As Los Angeles grew wealthier, it developed a richer cultural scene. Concert halls and opera houses opened downtown. Music societies hosted orchestras, choirs, and visiting artists. Some theaters specialized in vaudeville, while others moved into the exciting new world of silent film screenings. On weekends, families might go "downtown" to shop at department stores, see a show, or enjoy a meal at one of the city's restaurants.

Sports and Outdoor Activities

Sports gained popularity. **Baseball** was played in local leagues, and some bigger teams visited on barnstorming tours. Track and field meets, bicycle races, and boxing matches drew crowds. The city's mild weather allowed for year-round outdoor fun, from tennis to simple picnics in the park. Families traveled by streetcar to beaches, where swimming, fishing, and strolling on piers became weekend traditions.

---

15. Architecture and Urban Planning

Styles of the Era

Downtown Los Angeles and nearby neighborhoods showcased diverse architectural styles in the early 1900s. Some buildings had **Victorian** touches, with ornate trim and steep roofs. Others embraced the **Mission Revival** style, echoing Spanish missions with stucco walls and red tile roofs. Wealthy residents in areas like **West Adams** built grand homes with columns and large porches.

City Beautiful Movement

A national trend called the **City Beautiful Movement** influenced local planners. They believed that attractive boulevards, public buildings, and parks could promote civic pride and social harmony. Though Los Angeles did not fully remake itself as some eastern cities did, a few projects aimed to beautify the downtown area with tree-lined streets and classical-inspired civic buildings. Public squares and monuments were discussed, though many dreams remained on paper for lack of funds.

16. Transportation Challenges and Road Building

Congestion on Streets

With the growth of both streetcars and automobiles, downtown streets became crowded by the 1910s. The narrow roads, built for horse traffic decades earlier, could not easily handle large numbers of cars, trucks, wagons, and trolleys. Traffic jams occurred, especially during busy hours. Pedestrians dodged vehicles while crossing. Calls rose for better traffic control—stop signs, signals, and dedicated lanes.

Early Highway Projects

Seeing the future in autos, some county leaders proposed **parkways**—scenic roads that could carry faster car traffic. Though many Angelenos still relied on streetcars, advocates for highways argued that roads were more flexible and convenient. By the 1920s, the seeds of a future freeway system were planted, though actual freeways would not appear until later. Yet even in this era, you could sense that Los Angeles might become a car-focused place, as expansions of roads were frequently on the city council's agenda.

17. The Impact of World War I

Wartime Production

When World War I broke out in 1914 (the U.S. joined in 1917), Los Angeles factories that produced steel parts, tires, and other goods got more business supplying military equipment. The port area saw more shipbuilding activity. Thousands of new workers arrived to fill these jobs. The city supported war bond drives, and local newspapers urged citizens to conserve food and materials for the troops.

Social Effects

With many young men drafted, women took on roles in factories or offices. This shift built on the growing acceptance of women in the workforce. After the war ended in 1918, some women kept their jobs, but many returned home or faced pressure to do so. The war also brought global influenza in 1918–1919, which sickened many Angelenos. The city imposed quarantines, closed schools and theaters for weeks. Though it was a difficult time, Los Angeles emerged from the war with an even larger industrial base and population.

18. Cultural Clashes and Moral Campaigns

Prohibition and Reform Movements

In the 1910s, moral reform movements gained ground. Temperance groups had long pushed for banning alcohol, blaming it for crime and broken families. Los Angeles had active chapters that campaigned tirelessly. By 1920, national **Prohibition** became law, making the sale of alcoholic beverages illegal. This led to underground bars (speakeasies) and bootlegging operations in Los Angeles, as in many U.S. cities. Police tried to enforce the ban, but corruption and secret deals were common.

Anti-Vice Campaigns

Other campaigns targeted gambling, prostitution, and "immoral" films or shows. Civic leaders worried that the city's fast growth would attract crime. They closed some dance halls and censored certain theatrical acts. At the same time, Hollywood's early film production faced scrutiny from local churches and conservative groups, who insisted that movies meet moral standards. This tension between free expression and moral policing became a recurring theme in Los Angeles culture.

19. Stepping Toward Modernity

Shifting from Agriculture

While citrus and other farms still surrounded Los Angeles, new suburbs kept paving over farmland. Real estate developers saw bigger profits in housing. Factories, oil fields, and film studios also sought land, gradually chipping away at orange groves. Some orchard owners sold out for good money, moving to more rural corners of Southern California or leaving agriculture altogether. The city's face was changing from rural farmland to an urban and industrial mix.

Building a Reputation

By the mid-1920s, Los Angeles was nationally known as a growing city of possibilities—good climate, new jobs, and an expanding cultural scene. Promoters boasted of modern department stores, wide streets, and the glamorous potential of the film industry. Although many of these claims were a bit exaggerated, the city did exhibit a blend of old and new that captured the country's imagination. Visitors marveled at the palm-lined boulevards, the shining new buildings, and the sense that Los Angeles represented the future.

20. Chapter Conclusion

By the 1920s, Los Angeles had evolved dramatically from its days as a small pueblo:

1. **Population Boom:** Swelling ranks transformed the city into a diverse, vibrant hub.
2. **Transportation Shifts:** Electric streetcars and early automobiles competed to define travel, while railroads remained vital for freight.
3. **Government Growth:** City services expanded—paving streets, building sewers, and regulating health. Annexations enlarged the city's territory.
4. **Industrial and Oil Expansion:** Factories and oil fields diversified the economy beyond agriculture.
5. **Cultural Mosaic:** Immigrant communities enriched the city's life with new foods, languages, and celebrations, while tension over race and labor surfaced.
6. **Education and Reform:** Schools, women's suffrage, and moral campaigns shaped daily life and politics.
7. **Approach to Modern Times:** Farmers sold orchard land to developers, film studios took root, and boosters proclaimed Los Angeles a city of the future.

All these changes laid the groundwork for the next big debates—particularly about water. As the city grew, it needed more resources, most critically a stable water supply. In the coming years, fierce struggles over water rights and ambitious engineering would redefine both the city and its relationship with surrounding regions. We will explore that pivotal story next, in **Chapter 14**, focusing on the **Water Wars** and how they fueled more city expansion.

CHAPTER 14

Water Wars and City Expansion

Even in its early days, Los Angeles wrestled with limited water supplies. By the 20th century, this problem had become urgent. As the population exploded, the Los Angeles River and local groundwater could no longer meet the city's needs. City leaders turned to distant sources, sparking conflicts known as the **Water Wars**. In this chapter, we will examine why water was so crucial, how Los Angeles secured it, and the consequences for the city and those living in outlying regions. We will focus on events primarily in the early 1900s and 1910s, though later expansions and disputes also matter in understanding the city's history.

1. Background: Thirsty City in a Dry Land

Rainfall Realities

Los Angeles has a Mediterranean-like climate, with mild, wet winters and hot, dry summers. Annual rainfall can be unpredictable—some years bring heavy storms, while others see drought. As the city's population soared above 100,000 and then 200,000, the old **zanja** system and local wells proved insufficient. City officials knew they had to find more water or face a development standstill.

The Role of the Los Angeles River

The **Los Angeles River** had been the main water source since the Pueblo de Los Ángeles was founded in 1781. However, it was small and often prone to flooding in winter or running low in summer. As farmland spread and people drilled more wells, groundwater levels dropped. By 1900, the city recognized that local supplies could not support further growth. If Los Angeles wanted to become a major metropolis, it needed a new plan—and soon.

2. The Search for New Water Sources

William Mulholland

One of the key figures in the city's water strategy was **William Mulholland**, an immigrant from Ireland who rose through the ranks of the Los Angeles Water Department. Mulholland was self-taught in engineering and had a single-minded vision: secure a reliable water supply, no matter the distance or difficulty. He believed that with enough planning and construction, the city could tap into rivers far beyond its immediate basin.

Mulholland famously said, "If you don't get the water, you won't need it," suggesting that without water, growth would grind to a halt and people would leave. Backed by city leaders and real estate boosters, Mulholland became the driving force behind an audacious project: bringing water from the distant **Owens Valley**, over 200 miles away, to Los Angeles.

Eyeing the Owens Valley

The **Owens River** flows east of the Sierra Nevada Mountains in a sparsely populated area known as the Owens Valley. Fed by mountain snowmelt, it waters farmland there and empties into Owens Lake (which, by the early 1900s, was already shrinking due to irrigation diversions). Mulholland and his allies saw the Owens River as an abundant supply for a city that had few other options. But first, they needed to secure rights to that water—a process that proved controversial and secretive.

---

3. The Politics of the Owens Valley

Purchasing Land and Water Rights

Around 1905, agents working for Los Angeles quietly bought up ranches, farms, and water rights in the Owens Valley. They did not openly say they represented the city. Instead, they portrayed themselves as private investors or local speculators. Farmers who sold their properties often felt they had made a fair deal at the time, only to learn later that the land was actually part of a scheme to divert the river to Los Angeles.

This secrecy ignited anger. Critics accused the city of trickery. Owens Valley residents felt they had been misled into selling their lifeblood—the water feeding their crops and communities. But Los Angeles leaders argued that the purchases were legal and necessary. They pointed out that the city was paying for the land and water rights, not stealing them.

Federal Support

The federal government played a role, too. Leaders like President Theodore Roosevelt favored big water projects in the West, believing irrigation and reservoir construction would spur development. The Bureau of Reclamation, a federal agency, originally planned to help local Owens Valley farmers build irrigation works. But that plan stalled once Los Angeles gained key rights in the valley. Eventually, federal officials sided with the city or stepped aside, enabling the project to move forward.

---

4. Building the Los Angeles Aqueduct

Engineering Marvel

Constructing the **Los Angeles Aqueduct** was a massive undertaking. Surveyors plotted a route from the Owens Valley, over mountains and across deserts, to the city. Workers drilled **tunnels** through solid rock, built **concrete channels**, and erected siphons to carry water uphill in certain spots. Completed in 1913, the aqueduct stretched about 233 miles and took six years to build. It used gravity to move water, meaning no expensive pumping stations were needed (except in small cases). This design lowered operating costs but required precise engineering to maintain the flow.

When the aqueduct opened, Mulholland famously declared, "There it is. Take it." as water flowed into the city's reservoirs for the first time. It was a triumphant moment for Los Angeles leaders, who saw the aqueduct as proof of the city's destiny to become a great metropolis.

Worker Conditions

As with rail construction, the aqueduct project relied on crews of laborers working in tough conditions—extreme heat in the desert, cold winters in the mountains, and dangerous tunneling. Many were immigrants or seasonal workers. Accidents, rockfalls, and illness claimed lives. Yet the promise of steady wages and the sense of building something historic attracted many men to the job. When the aqueduct was finished, it stood as one of the largest public water projects in the world at that time.

5. Consequences for the Owens Valley

Drying Farmland

The arrival of the aqueduct spelled trouble for Owens Valley's agriculture. As Los Angeles diverted more water, local rivers and streams diminished. Farms that once grew alfalfa, fruits, and other crops withered. Ranches that depended on the Owens River found it shrinking or gone. Angry valley residents accused Los Angeles of turning their region into a dust bowl. Over time, Owens Lake dried out, leaving a salty, dusty lakebed that caused windblown dust storms.

Resistance and Conflict

Owens Valley residents did not quietly accept their fate. In the 1920s, they staged protests and even acts of sabotage, blowing up sections of the aqueduct. Although these attacks caused temporary interruptions in water flow, Los Angeles had the legal rights and the money to repair damages quickly. The city also built new infrastructure to grab more water, leading to ongoing resentment in the valley. This clash was a true **"Water War,"** pitting a growing urban center against a rural community fighting for its survival.

6. How the Aqueduct Fueled Los Angeles' Expansion

Confidence for Developers

With a large, reliable water supply in place, real estate developers felt more secure about building housing tracts, factories, and businesses. "We have the water," they boasted. Subdivisions sprawled outward, offering new residents a piece of sunny Southern California. As farmland near the city converted to housing, new farmland sprang up in outlying areas, also served by aqueduct water.

Thus, the aqueduct became a selling point: no longer did people worry that Los Angeles might run out of water in a dry year. Banks lent money more freely, fueling construction booms. Population soared: from about 320,000 in 1910 to over 570,000 by 1920, and it kept climbing. This was partly thanks to the aqueduct's assurance that water would be available for domestic use, businesses, and agriculture.

Industrial Growth

Factories and businesses also needed water. Oil refineries, metal works, canneries, and chemical plants used enormous quantities. Thanks to the Owens Valley water, the city could promise a steady supply. This advantage made Los Angeles more competitive with other cities. Ports along the coast handled increasing freight, as raw materials arrived and finished goods were shipped out. The synergy of water, rail, and harbor facilities propelled the region's industrial rise.

7. Mulholland's Legacy and Further Projects

Celebrated Engineer

For many Angelenos, William Mulholland became a hero—an engineer who had solved the city's biggest problem. Streets, schools, and landmarks bore his name. He commanded respect among political leaders and newspapers. Critics in the Owens Valley labeled him a villain, but in Los Angeles, he was largely admired. His achievements symbolized the city's can-do spirit: a willingness to tackle huge challenges through engineering prowess.

Plans for More Water

Mulholland did not stop with the Owens Valley aqueduct. He recognized that as Los Angeles continued growing, even that supply might not be enough. Surveys were made to tap rivers in Northern California, or possibly the Colorado River. Over the next decades, these ideas turned into major projects like the **Colorado River Aqueduct** (constructed in the 1930s). But in the early 1900s to 1920s, the Owens Valley system was the main triumph—and controversy.

8. City Boundaries Expand Further

Annexations Continue

With a stable water source, Los Angeles resumed annexing nearby lands and towns. Many smaller communities voted to join the city so they could gain access to the aqueduct water. Places that had once struggled with wells or small local systems saw the advantage of hooking into a large municipal supply. From 1910 to 1930, Los Angeles' area grew many times over, swallowing suburbs across the San Fernando Valley and beyond.

City leaders often used water as a bargaining chip: "Join Los Angeles, and you'll get water for growth." This strategy worked well. Some critics called it coercion; supporters said it was necessary to build a unified metropolis. Regardless, the city's footprint became one of the largest in the nation.

The San Fernando Valley Acquisition

One especially notable annexation was the **San Fernando Valley** in 1915. Real estate interests and politicians quietly bought large tracts of valley land before the aqueduct was complete, then sold them at higher prices once they secured city water. This scandal became part of the city's growth story—yet it didn't stop the annexation. Residents in the Valley eventually voted to join Los Angeles, spurred by the promise of aqueduct water for drinking and farming. Over time, the Valley transformed from ranchland into a sprawling suburban region.

9. The Changing Environment

Owens Lake Desiccation

As water was diverted, **Owens Lake** almost entirely dried out, revealing a salty lakebed prone to fierce dust storms. These storms caused health and environmental problems, scattering fine particles across the valley. Wildlife habitats vanished, and local fish populations declined drastically. This damage echoed the broader cost of urban water demands on distant ecosystems.

Local Ecological Impacts

Meanwhile, increased water in Los Angeles changed local ecosystems. Water was channeled into city pipes and away from the Los Angeles River, which saw sections turned into storm drains. Over time, the river's natural flow decreased, altering habitats for fish and birds. On the other hand, city parks and gardens flourished with imported water, introducing non-native plants that thrived in a mild climate. The city's greenery became a symbol of prosperity, though it masked deeper changes to the natural landscape.

---

10. Protests and Legal Battles

Owens Valley Strikes Back

From the 1920s onward, Owens Valley residents engaged in repeated protests. A group called the **Owens Valley Irrigation District** formed to fight for farmers' water rights. Armed men sometimes sabotaged the aqueduct, dynamiting gates or tunnels. Though the city repaired these breaks, the conflict remained bitter. The press sometimes labeled these saboteurs as criminals, while valley supporters saw them as freedom fighters defending their homes.

Court Disputes

Lawsuits flew back and forth. Owens Valley interests claimed Los Angeles had violated earlier agreements or misused water rights. The city argued it had legally purchased them and that the valley's development was not feasible without more advanced irrigation techniques. Judges often sided with Los Angeles, though some rulings forced the city to release small amounts of water back into local creeks. Over decades, the legal wrangling continued, shaping a legacy of mistrust between the city and valley.

11. Benefits for Los Angeles Residents

Reliable Water at Home

For ordinary Angelenos, the aqueduct meant turning on a tap and getting reliable water—an immense change from the days of uncertain wells or rationed supplies. Indoor plumbing became standard in new houses, and older homes upgraded. Streets had enough water for cleaning and fighting fires, and public health improved as a result. City officials boasted that Los Angeles would never run dry again.

Economic Boom

Businesses also thrived thanks to a stable water supply. Factories, refineries, and commercial enterprises could plan expansions without worrying about water shortages. The city's national reputation grew, attracting more migrants. Real estate soared, with land prices climbing each time new water lines reached a neighborhood. This synergy of water and growth fed the notion that Los Angeles was a city of limitless opportunity.

12. Criticism of Imperial Ambitions

Debates Over "Stealing Water"

Not everyone hailed the Owens Valley project as heroic. Journalists, environmentalists, and some politicians condemned it as "stealing water" from a rural community. They argued that Los Angeles had used underhanded tactics, disguised deals, and political power to grab a resource it had no moral right to exploit. This viewpoint painted the city as an imperial force, willing to ruin distant lands for its own gain.

City boosters responded that the water was purchased legally and that the city's growth benefited the entire region economically. They insisted that the Owens Valley was better suited for ranching on a smaller scale, not large-scale agriculture. Meanwhile, valley residents felt betrayed and angry, fueling a story of David versus Goliath that persisted in local lore.

---

13. Engineers and Visionaries

Beyond Mulholland

William Mulholland was not alone in shaping Los Angeles' water story. Other engineers, such as **Fred Eaton** (a former mayor of Los Angeles), played crucial roles in the negotiations for Owens Valley land. Eaton's behind-the-scenes work set the stage for Mulholland's engineering feats. Over time, younger engineers joined the city's water department, continuing expansions of pipes, reservoirs, and pumping stations.

Infrastructure Pride

The success of the aqueduct and later projects fed a strong engineering culture in Los Angeles. Locals took pride in their ability to build roads, aqueducts, and electric rail lines in challenging terrains. This mindset influenced how the city tackled future challenges, from flood control to freeway construction. The idea that "big projects can solve big problems" became part of Los Angeles' identity, for better or worse.

---

14. The St. Francis Dam Disaster

In 1928, a tragic event shook the faith in Mulholland's expertise: the **St. Francis Dam** in the San Francisquito Canyon, north of Los Angeles, collapsed shortly after completion. A massive flood of water rushed downstream, killing over 400 people. Investigations revealed possible design and geological flaws. Mulholland bore moral responsibility, stating, "The only ones I envy in this whole thing are the dead," and retired soon after. The disaster underscored the risks of large-scale water engineering. Yet it did not halt the city's determination to secure even more water from afar.

---

15. Ripple Effects on Local Politics

Power of the Water Department

By controlling the lifeblood of the city, the water department (and later the Department of Water and Power) gained immense influence. Decisions on where water lines went could boost property values. Politicians who cooperated with water department leaders had an edge. Critics alleged corruption or favoritism, but many residents simply wanted more water projects to keep up with demand.

Shaping City Elections

The aqueduct battles also affected how residents voted. Some politicians ran on platforms of further annexations and new aqueducts, while opponents demanded more transparency and fairness. While big business and real estate interests generally supported expansions, a few reformers questioned whether the city was growing too fast. Still, the overall momentum favored pro-water, pro-growth candidates.

---

16. Social Impact on Owens Valley Migrants

Leaving the Dry Land

As farming in Owens Valley became more difficult, many families moved away, some heading to Los Angeles for work in factories or to other

California farming areas with reliable irrigation. Their departure was a forced migration of sorts, driven by water scarcity. They arrived in Los Angeles carrying resentment and stories of betrayal, but also a need for new livelihoods.

Cultural Memory

For decades, the Owens Valley conflict remained a bitter memory passed down through families. Folk songs, poems, and local newsletters told of green fields lost and a lake turned to dust. In Los Angeles, awareness of the valley's suffering was low. People enjoyed turning on the tap, rarely thinking about the source. Only decades later would some Angelenos question the ethics of that "great water grab."

---

17. Further Water Sources and Plans

The Colorado River Idea

Even as the Owens Valley aqueduct came online, forward-thinkers recognized that a single source might not suffice for a city that could one day have millions of people. Talks turned to the **Colorado River**, which flows along California's eastern border. Eventually, in the 1930s, Los Angeles joined forces with other Southern California cities to build the Colorado River Aqueduct. This was after our immediate time frame but showed the continuing strategy: looking outward for water to fuel further expansion.

Local Storage and Dams

Within the region, more **dams** were proposed to capture local rainfall and store water from the aqueduct. Reservoirs like **Silver Lake**, **Hollywood**, and **Chatsworth** played roles in distributing the Owens water. The city water system became a complex network of pipes, tunnels, and storage basins. Engineers tinkered with ways to recharge groundwater basins with stormwater, though large-scale groundwater recharge was still in its infancy.

---

18. Cultural Representations

In Popular Media

Though not as famous as Hollywood's glitz, the Owens Valley conflict sometimes appeared in local newspapers, novels, and plays. Later films, like "Chinatown" (1974), would dramatize a fictionalized version of these events (though set in a slightly different era). Such stories hinted at the behind-the-scenes deals, corruption, and heartbreak that accompanied Los Angeles' growth. While "Chinatown" is set in the 1930s, it borrowed heavily from real tensions of the earlier Water Wars.

School Lessons

By the 1920s, local textbooks briefly mentioned the city's "triumph of engineering," praising the aqueduct as a marvel. They rarely highlighted the suffering of the Owens Valley. Over time, a few teachers added more balanced perspectives, but for a generation, many Angelenos believed the official narrative: Los Angeles was an innovative city that "brought water to the desert," ignoring or downplaying the negative side.

---

19. Lasting Effects on City Expansion

Enabling Suburbia

With water secured, suburban development boomed in the 1920s and beyond. Neighborhoods with single-family homes, lawns, and tree-lined streets spread across former farmland and open hills. This low-density pattern became a hallmark of Los Angeles. Had the city lacked sufficient water, it might have been forced to grow more densely or remain smaller.

Foundation for Future Battles

The success of the Owens Valley project also laid a template for how Los Angeles might approach future resources—seeking them from distant places. This approach would shape the region's environmental and political challenges for decades. Critics later argued that Los Angeles needed to learn conservation and manage resources more wisely instead of looking outward. Yet in this era, outward expansion was the norm.

20. Chapter Conclusion

The **Water Wars** of the early 1900s forever changed Los Angeles and Owens Valley:

1. **Urgent Need:** Rapid population growth forced city leaders to seek water beyond local sources.
2. **Mulholland's Vision:** William Mulholland engineered the ambitious Owens Valley Aqueduct, completed in 1913.
3. **Secret Deals and Anger:** L.A. agents quietly purchased water rights, leaving Owens Valley farmers feeling tricked.
4. **Aqueduct Triumph:** The project provided enough water for the city to keep expanding, fueling real estate booms, industrial growth, and annexations.
5. **Valley's Loss:** Owens Valley agriculture suffered; the lake dried up, dust storms rose, and local residents fought back with protests and sabotage.
6. **Urban Success vs. Rural Pain:** Los Angeles praised the aqueduct as a technological feat, while the valley saw it as a theft of their lifeblood.

7. **Model for Future Projects:** The conflict set a pattern of looking outward for resources, shaping the city's environmental and political challenges.
8. **Legacy and Lessons:** Although the city thrived, the ethics of water acquisition remained a question that future generations would revisit.

Having examined these water struggles, we see how they directly fueled greater expansion, transforming Los Angeles into a sprawling metropolis with growing influence. This era of engineering boldness and controversial resource grabbing set the stage for the city's next big phase. In the upcoming chapters, we will explore **oil booms**, the rise of **Hollywood**, and how Los Angeles navigated the **Great Depression** and beyond—still keeping most of our attention on earlier times, but hinting at how these events laid foundations for the modern city.

CHAPTER 15

Oil Boom and Rapid Growth

By the early 20th century, Los Angeles had a stable water supply (thanks to the Owens Valley aqueduct), a growing population, and expanding rail and streetcar networks. These factors set the stage for another major transformation: the **oil boom**. In this chapter, we will explore how new oil discoveries shaped Los Angeles' economy, skyline, and neighborhoods. We will see how drilling rigs popped up in unexpected places, bringing both wealth and problems. This period of rapid growth further changed the city from a semi-rural place to a more industrial and urban center—long before the glitz of Hollywood took center stage.

1. Early Oil Discoveries Revisited

The First Wells

Los Angeles was not completely new to oil. As we saw earlier, small wells existed in the late 1800s, especially in areas like Echo Park and near downtown. Early entrepreneurs recognized that Southern California's tar seeps (such as the La Brea Tar Pits) hinted at underground petroleum. However, these first attempts were modest, and many Angelenos still believed the region's main future lay in farming, citrus, and real estate.

Turn-of-the-Century Exploration

Around 1900, more sophisticated methods for locating and drilling oil began appearing. Engineers and geologists studied rock formations, drilled deeper wells, and developed better pumping equipment. Speculators formed small oil companies or partnered with established firms to explore neighborhoods, beaches, and open fields. As the city grew, demand for fuel rose too—trains, factories, and a tiny but increasing number of automobiles all needed oil or its byproducts.

2. The Gusher at Signal Hill

A Dramatic Discovery

One of the most important moments in the Los Angeles oil story occurred at **Signal Hill**, near Long Beach, in 1921. Drilling crews struck an enormous petroleum deposit, and the well erupted—a true "gusher" shooting oil high into the air. This dramatic sight captured headlines and spurred a rush of new drilling in the area. Within months, Signal Hill was covered with wooden derricks standing close together, each seeking its share of the black gold.

The Signal Hill find proved that Southern California had some of the richest oil fields in the country. Soon, the region's output rivaled major oil-producing states like Texas and Oklahoma. Wealth poured in, supporting local banks, real estate deals, and city projects. Overnight millionaires appeared, fueling tales of quick fortunes. Yet this quick wealth also brought chaos and environmental messes.

Wooden Forest of Derricks

Journalists described Signal Hill as a "wooden forest" because so many oil derricks dotted the land. At the peak, it seemed every available patch of ground had a rig. Some wells were just yards apart, occasionally causing technical problems or fights over drilling rights. The constant noise of pumps and the smell of crude oil filled the air. Workers lived in makeshift camps or boarding houses. Their labor was dangerous—blowouts, fires, or toxic fumes were constant risks. Despite these hazards, the chance to earn good wages attracted laborers from across the region.

---

3. Expansion of Oil Fields Across the City

The Inglewood Oil Field

Even before Signal Hill's success, other promising fields were found. The **Inglewood Oil Field** in southwestern Los Angeles grew quickly in the 1920s.

Derricks sprang up near what is now Baldwin Hills and around the city of Inglewood. Roads built for drilling crews later served new residential developments. Once farmland or grazing land, these rolling hills became an industrial zone with pump jacks nodding day and night.

Venice, Wilmington, and Beyond

Smaller oil fields appeared around Venice Beach, Wilmington (near the harbor), and sections of the San Fernando Valley. In some cases, oil rigs stood awkwardly close to homes, schools, or businesses. Residents who tolerated the inconvenience and smell might gain royalties if wells were on their property. Others fumed about pollution, noise, and the fear of accidents. Los Angeles was turning into a patchwork of neighborhoods and oil fields, blending residential life with heavy industry in ways rarely seen elsewhere.

---

4. Economic Impact and Job Creation

Boosting Local Wealth

The oil boom pumped vast amounts of money into the city. Oil companies paid taxes to local governments, which used the revenue for roads, public buildings, and utilities. Banks financed drilling operations, opening new branches. Entrepreneurs used profits to invest in real estate, expanding suburban tracts and downtown construction. The city's economy diversified, no longer leaning solely on agriculture, tourism, or real estate speculation.

Because of oil, many Angelenos found steady work as drillers, tool pushers, geologists, or refinery workers. Factories that refined or processed petroleum byproducts employed hundreds. While large oil companies (like Standard Oil or Union Oil) took the lion's share of profits, smaller local operators also thrived. Wealth from oil underwrote philanthropic projects—some wealthy oilmen funded civic improvements or cultural institutions, seeking social prestige.

Growth in Manufacturing

Cheap, plentiful oil encouraged more **manufacturing**. Factories found it easier to power machinery, and trucking fleets grew. Railroads still carried freight, but trucks could handle shorter local routes. This flexibility spurred the rise of distribution centers and warehouses across the city. Meanwhile, chemical plants emerged to produce plastics, fertilizers, and other petroleum-based products. Los Angeles was becoming a hub of industrial activity, spurred by the black gold beneath its feet.

---

5. Environmental and Neighborhood Conflicts

Pollution and Fires

Los Angeles discovered that oil production brought serious environmental problems. Spilled crude from poorly managed wells seeped into soil, damaging crops or gardens. Gases vented from wells caused foul odors and potential health risks. Occasionally, drilling rigs caught fire, sending black smoke billowing overhead. Harbor areas dealt with oil slicks along the water. Complaints from homeowners multiplied as new derricks encroached on residential streets.

Fire departments and city officials struggled to set safety standards. They introduced regulations for well spacing, containment pits, and waste disposal. But enforcement was uneven, especially in neighborhoods with lower incomes or less political power. Oil companies often had the upper hand, arguing that tight rules would hurt the city's prosperity.

Community Resistance

In some districts, local groups formed to fight new drilling. They lobbied the city council to ban rigs near homes or schools. Over time, certain areas adopted zoning laws limiting or prohibiting oil wells, pushing them to more industrial zones. Yet these battles were hard-fought. Many city leaders sided with oil interests, seeing them as crucial to Los Angeles' rapid growth. Thus, the city's shape—where industrial zones ended and residential zones began—often depended on who had the influence to protect their neighborhood from drilling.

6. The Role of Speculation and Land Deals

Buying and Selling Mineral Rights

Mineral rights—ownership of what lay beneath the surface—became a hot topic. A landowner might sell or lease the rights to an oil company, earning royalty payments on any oil extracted. Speculators bought up cheap land, hoping a discovery would make them rich. Sometimes, they subdivided land into small parcels, each sold with a promise of future oil. Many small investors lost money if wells turned out dry.

These speculative deals could lead to boom-and-bust cycles. A rumor of an upcoming strike would drive land prices up, then if the well disappointed, prices crashed. Unscrupulous promoters sometimes sold worthless shares in "paper" oil companies, tricking gullible buyers. City officials tried to warn the public about fraud, but the mania for oil investments was hard to quell when success stories were so visible.

Shaping Urban Form

Because many property owners hoped for an oil find, drilling rigs sometimes appeared in unexpected spots—parking lots, backyards, or even church grounds. If a well succeeded, the owner might finance major building projects or expansions. In other cases, speculation left half-finished developments or vacant lots where no oil was found. This uneven pattern contributed to the city's patchwork development, with some blocks bustling with rigs and heavy traffic, while adjacent blocks remained quiet.

---

7. Changing Skyline and Infrastructure

Tall Structures and Oil Towers

Before skyscrapers became common, wooden oil derricks rose above one- or two-story buildings. People traveling by train or car saw these spindly towers from afar, signaling the region's new wealth. Eventually, steel derricks replaced wood, especially for deeper wells. Though these rigs were purely functional, they reshaped the visual identity of parts of Los Angeles. Tourists sometimes visited drill sites, marveling at the machines pumping black liquid from the ground.

Refineries and Pipelines

Crude oil had to be processed into gasoline, kerosene, and other products. Refineries clustered in places like El Segundo, Wilmington, and other harbor areas. Pipelines snaked across the city to carry crude to these refineries. Workers built large storage tanks, shipping terminals, and rail sidings. At night, flares from refinery stacks lit up the sky. The pungent smell of refining hung in the air, especially on still, warm days. This industrial web further reinforced Los Angeles' growing status as a major energy center.

---

8. Labor Relations in the Oil Industry

Workers and Wages

Oil field work paid better than many other jobs, but it was dangerous and physically demanding. Roughnecks (rig hands), drillers, and other crew members toiled in extreme heat or cold, often covered in oil and mud. They risked blowouts, fires, and accidents with heavy equipment. In the 1920s, wages were decent enough to attract men from rural areas or other parts of the country. Some found the oil fields an opportunity to climb the social ladder if they saved money or invested wisely.

Union Efforts

A few labor unions tried to organize oil workers, seeking safer conditions and fair hours. Companies resisted, fearing strikes could halt production and cost them profits. Small-scale walkouts or protests did occur, but union membership in the oil sector remained limited compared to other industries. Many workers were transient, moving from one oil boom town to another. This lack of stable roots made collective organizing harder.

---

9. Financial Titans and Political Influence

Rise of Oil Barons

Just as the railroad era had its "railroad barons," the oil boom produced a new elite. Wealthy oilmen funded local newspapers, supported friendly politicians, and shaped city policy. They might donate land for parks or sponsor civic events, hoping to gain public favor. Some joined boards of banks or charities, cementing their status in high society. This new money class sometimes clashed with older families who had made fortunes in real estate or agriculture, each group vying for influence.

Impact on City Hall

Politicians who backed the oil industry found campaign support and financial backing. In turn, they passed or blocked legislation regarding drilling regulations, zoning, or taxes. Critics alleged corruption and backroom deals. Some city council members or county supervisors openly acknowledged that oil revenue was critical to local government budgets, so they had to maintain a pro-industry stance. The result was a political climate that often favored development over environmental or neighborhood concerns.

---

10. Effects on Transportation and Roads

A Boost for Automobiles

As oil became abundant, gasoline prices dropped, encouraging more Angelenos to consider buying a car. While we covered the early car culture in the previous chapter, the oil boom now made fuel cheaper and more accessible. Service stations (gas stations) popped up along main roads, further easing the transition from horse-drawn vehicles and streetcars to private autos. This shift laid the foundation for the deeper car culture that would later define Los Angeles.

Improved Roads

With new tax revenue from oil, city and county officials paved more streets and built better highways. Oil companies sometimes donated asphalt (a petroleum product) for road surfacing, promoting the idea that improved roads would also help them move equipment or transport supplies. Better roads helped connect suburban areas, making it easier for families to commute or shop in distant parts of town. This slow but steady improvement in roads weakened the streetcar's dominance, though that system was still strong in the 1920s.

11. Oil Exports and the Port of Los Angeles

Harbor Development

Los Angeles Harbor at San Pedro and Wilmington expanded rapidly to handle tanker ships exporting oil or importing drilling equipment. Dredging operations deepened channels so larger vessels could dock. Rail spurs and cargo cranes multiplied along the waterfront. The city's harbor board partnered with shipping companies, creating new jobs in stevedoring and ship maintenance. Oil exports quickly became a major part of port activity.

International Markets

Once refined, California petroleum products were sold not only across the United States but also to markets in Asia and Latin America. American companies, sometimes with local offices in Los Angeles, arranged global deals. Tankers left the port loaded with fuel for distant ports. This gave Los Angeles an international footprint, raising its profile as a major city on the Pacific Rim, even though it was not yet the giant metropolis it would become.

12. Cultural Reflections of the Oil Boom

Literature and Films

Writers and journalists captured the drama of gushers and the gritty life of oil field workers. Some local newspapers featured stories of rags-to-riches success or tragic accidents on the rigs. While the broader film industry was just beginning to blossom, a few silent movies showed oil scenes for dramatic effect. Later decades would see more cinematic takes on the oil business, but seeds were planted in this era, shaping a popular image of wildcatters chasing fortune.

Public Perception

Many residents were proud that Los Angeles was no longer a sleepy citrus town. They pointed to the oil fields as proof of modern progress. However, some worried about the city losing its charm amid drilling noise, pollution, and industrial sprawl. Travel magazines of the 1920s offered conflicting images: sunny beaches and orange groves on one page, smoky refineries and pump jacks on another. The city's identity was in flux, blending romance and reality.

13. Unintended Consequences and Earthquakes

Ground Subsidence

Extracting large quantities of oil and gas from underground can cause the ground to sink, a phenomenon known as **subsidence**. Parts of the

Wilmington and Long Beach areas experienced this. Buildings developed cracks, roads buckled, and utility lines broke. Residents demanded solutions—filling wells, injecting water to stabilize the ground, or limiting extraction rates. Oil companies resisted, worried about profits, but eventually, some measures were put in place to slow subsidence.

Earthquake Fears

Southern California is seismically active. The added drilling and extraction of underground fluids raised questions about whether it could trigger more earthquakes or intensify existing faults. Scientists in the 1920s did not fully understand these processes, but news of small tremors near oil fields alarmed the public. While direct links between drilling and major quakes remained debated, the region's vulnerability added to concerns about the rapid exploitation of underground resources.

---

14. Shaping the Image of a "Modern" City

Electric Lights and Power

Oil money helped fund **electric power plants**, bridging gaps in the city's energy supply. The city and private companies built more lines for electric lighting, powering new streetlamps and electrified signage. Downtown Los Angeles gained a bright nightlife, with theaters and cafes staying open later. This "city of lights" effect bolstered the notion that Los Angeles was a modern hub, leaving behind the dusty darkness of older frontier towns.

Architecture and Finance

Downtown architecture advanced, too. Office buildings of reinforced concrete and steel soared to new heights (though city regulations limited building height for many years). Banks and insurance companies that handled oil revenue built grand structures, reflecting the city's rising confidence. Lobby murals or decorations sometimes celebrated industry, with images of drill rigs or ships. These visual cues told visitors that Los Angeles was not just about citrus and sunshine—it was an industrial powerhouse, too.

15. Conflicts with Tourism and Leisure

Balancing Industry and Fun

Los Angeles boosters still wanted to market the region as a sunny paradise of beaches and orange groves. Oil derricks on the shoreline conflicted with images of pristine sand. Beach towns like Venice or Long Beach had to decide how to zone their land—would they allow wells on or near the sand? Some did, for the revenue. Tourists might see pump jacks operating close to bathing areas, an odd mix of leisure and industry.

Over time, local chambers of commerce tried to hide the more unsightly aspects of oil extraction from tourist brochures. Some derricks near major roads were enclosed in decorative "false buildings" or disguised as towers. This trend would continue later, with wells hidden behind fences or disguised as buildings to preserve the region's carefully crafted image as a vacation spot.

Resort Towns Struggle

Communities that banked on tourism faced tough choices. Letting oil companies drill could bring quick wealth but might repel visitors looking for relaxation, fresh air, and scenic views. Some towns refused drilling permits near prime beach property, pushing wells inland. Others permitted it wholeheartedly, leading to short-term gains but potential long-term damage to their resort reputation. These contrasting approaches shaped the coastline's development, dividing beach areas into heavily industrialized stretches and more purely recreational ones.

---

16. Evolving Regulation and Industry Changes

Moves Toward Zoning

As the 1920s progressed, the city council experimented with **zoning laws** that separated residential, commercial, and industrial uses. Oil extraction often fell under industrial zoning. This was an early step in controlling the city's haphazard expansion. However, many existing wells were "grandfathered in," meaning they could keep operating even if new zoning rules prohibited them. This partial system created patchwork regulations that persisted for decades.

Shifting Oil Demand

At the same time, national and world markets for oil grew. Cars and trucks replaced horse-drawn vehicles in many American cities. Ships began converting from coal to oil power. Airplane engines also required petroleum. This rising demand meant Los Angeles oil fields remained profitable, though new fields in Texas, Oklahoma, and the Middle East eventually introduced competition. Over time, some older L.A. fields declined in output, forcing companies to drill deeper or move on.

---

17. Social Life in Oil Towns

Worker Camps and Culture

In areas like Signal Hill or the Inglewood Oil Field, small communities formed around the rigs. Workers and families lived in rough shacks or hastily built bungalows. Saloons, diners, and supply stores popped up, catering to the oil crowd. Some workers formed baseball teams or fraternal clubs to boost morale. Life was gritty, with long shifts and few amenities, but shared camaraderie.

Gender Roles

Men typically held the field jobs, while women managed households, cared for children, and sometimes worked in boarding houses or local shops. A few women entered clerical or bookkeeping roles for oil companies. Traditional gender roles still dominated, though the city's overall modernization allowed more women to find office work downtown or in business districts.

18. Tension Between Old and New Wealth

Agricultural Holdouts

Some longtime ranchers and orchard owners felt overshadowed by the new oil elite. They had shaped Los Angeles through citrus, but now the city's pride shifted to industrial might. Real estate developers or oil speculators sometimes looked down on small farmers as relics of a simpler past. Meanwhile, farmers who found oil on their property often sold out and moved on, leaving behind farmland for drilling or suburban tracts.

Cultural Shifts

Oil money funded new forms of entertainment and nightlife, accelerating the city's cultural transformation. Speakeasies (during Prohibition) thrived in some oil-boom neighborhoods. Fancy restaurants and hotels catered to oil executives. In older communities, traditions of rural life—rodeos, barn dances, harvest fairs—lost their appeal or shrank. Thus, the oil era eroded parts of the region's agricultural heritage, replacing them with an urban-industrial culture.

---

19. Setting the Stage for Future Changes

Prelude to Hollywood's Rise

Even though the film industry was growing, the city in the 1910s–1920s still relied heavily on oil revenue. This would shift when Hollywood exploded in the later 1920s and 1930s, but for now, black gold was the driving force behind Los Angeles' rapid expansion. The next chapter will delve deeply into how Hollywood and early filmmakers put Los Angeles on the global map in a new way.

Economic Diversification

Oil's success ensured that Los Angeles was no longer a one-trick pony. Combined with agriculture, manufacturing, shipping, and real estate, the city had multiple pillars of economic stability. This diversification helped Los Angeles weather financial storms that might have crippled regions relying on a single resource. However, it also meant the city had to balance conflicting interests—protecting farmland, hosting heavy industry, expanding tourism, and managing residential growth.

CHAPTER 16

Hollywood and the Early Film Era

While oil extraction reshaped the city's economy and skyline, a quieter revolution was taking place in the Los Angeles area—one that would eventually overshadow even black gold. **Hollywood**, once a small town with orange groves and dusty roads, was poised to become the heart of a global film empire. In this chapter, we will look at how the early film industry arrived, why it thrived in Southern California, and how it shaped the culture and landscape of Los Angeles before the Great Depression years.

1. Hollywood Before Movies

A Quaint Community

Originally, **Hollywood** was a rural settlement just northwest of downtown Los Angeles. In the late 1800s, it was known for its citrus groves, rolling hills, and a small population that appreciated the mild climate. When the town leaders agreed to be annexed by Los Angeles in 1910 (as discussed in Chapter 13), they did so partly to secure water and other city services. At that time, no one foresaw that Hollywood would become a movie capital.

Early Influences

Even before the major studios arrived, a few independent filmmakers trickled into the Los Angeles area around 1907–1910, escaping the high costs and patent lawsuits in New York and New Jersey. Sunny weather, varied landscapes (beaches, deserts, mountains), and cheaper land made Southern California appealing. They shot short "one-reelers" on borrowed ranches or city streets, impressing audiences with the region's bright, outdoor look. This planted the seeds for bigger productions.

2. Why Southern California?

Sunshine and Scenery

In the early 1900s, film technology required a lot of natural light. Indoor lighting systems were weak and unreliable, so outdoor filming was essential. Los Angeles offered **year-round sunshine**, reducing delays caused by bad weather. Also, the region's variety of landscapes—beach, mountain, forest, and desert—all within a short drive—gave filmmakers endless backdrops without traveling far.

Distance from Patent Wars

On the East Coast, Thomas Edison and others owned patents on camera equipment, leading to legal fights. Independent producers risked lawsuits or equipment seizures if they filmed back east. In Los Angeles, they were farther from Edison's reach, making it easier to experiment. Once local courts proved friendlier, more filmmakers moved west, drawn by the freedom to work outside Edison's dominance.

---

3. The First Studios

The Birth of a Local Industry

Around 1910, the **Biograph Company** sent a crew to Los Angeles to film "Ramona," featuring star Mary Pickford. They returned with glowing reports of the region's potential. Soon, **Essanay**, **Kalem**, and other small studios set up temporary offices. By 1912, producers such as **Carl Laemmle** (who later founded Universal Pictures) and **Jesse L. Lasky** were leasing or buying land for permanent facilities. Simple open-air stages, made of wood and canvas, allowed filming under natural sunlight.

These early "studios" were modest—some were just fenced lots with scattered buildings for dressing rooms and prop storage. But they quickly multiplied. In a few years, Hollywood had more than a dozen production outfits, each cranking out short silent films at a dizzying pace.

Universal City and Others

One milestone came in 1915, when Carl Laemmle opened **Universal City** in the San Fernando Valley, north of Hollywood. Billed as the largest motion picture production facility in the world, it had administrative offices, sets, stages, and even a zoo for exotic animals used in films. Tourists could pay a small fee to watch filmmaking in action. Soon after, **Paramount**, **Fox**, and other companies established or expanded their Hollywood presence, solidifying Los Angeles as film's new epicenter.

4. Silent Films and Rising Stars

The Silent Era

Films in the 1910s and early 1920s were silent, accompanied by live music in theaters. Title cards displayed dialogue or story points. Audiences were captivated by the moving images and the charisma of "picture personalities." Directors like D.W. Griffith innovated camera angles, close-ups, and epic storytelling. Though Griffith's "The Birth of a Nation" (1915) was controversial for racist themes, it proved film could be a massive commercial success, drawing huge crowds.

Celebrity Culture

The film industry created a new phenomenon: the movie star. **Charlie Chaplin**, with his "Little Tramp" persona, became a global icon. Mary Pickford, known as "America's Sweetheart," commanded high salaries and had a devoted fan base. Douglas Fairbanks thrilled audiences with swashbuckling roles. Fans clamored for autographs, gossip, and anything connected to these shining celebrities. Hollywood found that star power sold tickets—and fed the local economy.

5. Hollywood Transforms Los Angeles

Job Opportunities

As studios expanded, they hired carpenters to build sets, seamstresses to sew costumes, extras to fill crowd scenes, and technicians to operate cameras or lights. Local suppliers provided lumber, fabric, and props. Eager jobseekers arrived from across the country, hoping to break into the "pictures" in any capacity. Even if most never became stars, they contributed to the city's workforce and population growth.

Impact on Real Estate

Producers needed land for backlots and studios, fueling a demand for large parcels. Neighborhoods near these studios sprouted middle-class housing for employees. Star actors, flush with cash, built lavish homes in areas like **Beverly Hills** or the hills above Hollywood, setting trends for architectural styles—Spanish Colonial, Tudor, or Mediterranean. This helped shape Los Angeles as a city of distinct neighborhoods, each with its own flair.

---

6. The Studio System Emerges

Vertical Integration

By the 1920s, major studios consolidated their power. They controlled production (making the films), distribution (getting them to theaters), and exhibition (owning theater chains). This "vertical integration" meant a studio could cast stars under exclusive contracts, produce movies on its own stages, ship them to its own theaters, and keep most of the profits. Such a system allowed for stable, factory-like production schedules, with crews making multiple films at once.

Contract Players

Actors, directors, writers, and other talent often signed long-term contracts. A young starlet might earn a weekly salary under strict studio conditions—where to appear, how to dress, and even who to date for publicity stunts. Studios molded these personalities to fit specific on-screen images. While some actors thrived, others chafed under controlling executives or faced heavy pressure to remain "box-office friendly." Still, the promise of stardom kept new hopefuls arriving by train and bus every day.

7. The Hollywood Community Grows

Businesses and Services

With so many film workers around, Hollywood's main streets filled with restaurants, costume shops, beauty salons, and specialized stores selling props or camera gear. Agents and publicists set up offices to manage careers and press coverage. Photographers built studios for "glamour shots." Hotels near studio lots catered to out-of-towners visiting for auditions. In short, a whole ecosystem formed around the film industry.

Social Clubs and Nightlife

Stars and executives frequented exclusive clubs like the **Hollywood Athletic Club** or local speakeasies (during Prohibition). Parties sometimes took place in grand mansions, fueling gossip columns. Tourists from across the nation tried to catch glimpses of stars in restaurants or on the street. Hollywood nightlife combined with the city's broader modernization, creating a sense of excitement. But there was also disapproval from more conservative locals who disliked the fast living and rumored scandals.

8. Technological Advances

Better Cameras and Lights

As the silent era progressed, camera technology improved, allowing smoother tracking shots, better film stock sensitivity, and more consistent lighting. Studios built enclosed sound stages with skylights or electric lights for controlled filming. Inventors in Los Angeles contributed to these breakthroughs, turning the city into a hub for film tech. Skilled technicians formed the backbone of each production, learning new methods on the job.

Special Effects and Stunts

Stunt work advanced, too. Daredevil performers jumped from buildings, crashed cars, or wrestled with wild animals to amaze audiences. Special effects teams developed miniatures, matte paintings, or trick photography for illusions. Because of open spaces and varied terrain, studios could stage large-scale battle scenes or western showdowns. This high-octane approach to filmmaking became a hallmark of Hollywood's flair, drawing attention from global audiences.

---

9. Movie Palaces and Theaters

Ornate Architecture

With films becoming a prime form of entertainment, theater owners built grand "movie palaces." Downtown Los Angeles and Hollywood Boulevard gained venues like Grauman's Egyptian Theatre (1922) and Grauman's Chinese Theatre (1927). These theaters featured exotic decor (Egyptian, Chinese, Spanish styles), plush seating, and even air conditioning—a luxury at the time. Going to the movies became a glamorous event, not just a casual outing.

Community Theaters Everywhere

Beyond these flagship palaces, smaller neighborhood theaters popped up in suburbs. Families could watch the latest Charlie Chaplin comedy or Mary Pickford drama close to home. Ticket prices were affordable, and weekly changes in programming meant steady foot traffic. Some theaters had balconies and pipe organs for live musical accompaniment. This widespread distribution anchored film as a central pastime for Angelenos of all income levels.

10. Changing Social Norms

Fashion and Behavior

Movie stars set trends in clothing, hairstyles, and behavior. Women copied the bobbed hair of actress Louise Brooks. Men admired the dashing mustaches of Rudolph Valentino. On-screen romances pushed boundaries for kissing or affectionate scenes, influencing real-life dating norms. Critics worried about the "moral decay" caused by these modern styles, but younger generations embraced the excitement.

Racial Stereotypes and Exclusions

Hollywood's early films often reflected social prejudices. Asian, African American, and Latino actors were rarely given starring roles; if they appeared at all, they often portrayed stereotypes. White actors sometimes used makeup to play characters of other races (so-called "yellowface" or "blackface"). Though a few performers of color found minor success, the industry remained largely segregated. This mirrored the broader racial divides in Los Angeles housing and jobs.

---

11. The Influence of Censorship

Fears of Immorality

As films grew more popular, some civic and religious groups demanded regulations to protect audiences from "indecency." They objected to sexual innuendo, crime stories without moral lessons, or portrayals of drinking (especially during Prohibition). Various states passed censorship laws, and local boards sometimes cut or banned films. Hollywood studios worried about lost revenue.

The Hayes Office

In the early 1920s, studios formed the **Motion Picture Producers and Distributors of America (MPPDA)**, hiring former Postmaster General Will

H. Hays to oversee moral guidelines. While the strict **Production Code** would come later (1930s), seeds of self-censorship began in the 1920s. Hollywood tried to preempt government crackdowns by policing itself. This climate of caution influenced scripts, costumes, and plotlines, though some filmmakers still pushed boundaries.

12. The Dawn of Talkies

The Jazz Singer (1927)

Though silent films reigned for most of the decade, the release of **"The Jazz Singer"** in 1927 (by Warner Bros.) introduced synchronized sound segments and changed everything. While not fully "talking" throughout, the film's popular musical numbers showed audiences a glimpse of cinema's future. Other studios rushed to adopt sound technology, building sound stages with better acoustics and equipping theaters with speakers.

Hollywood's Adaptation

Silent-era stars who excelled at pantomime now faced the challenge of recording dialogue. Some voices did not match on-screen personas. Directors, writers, and technicians scrambled to learn microphone placement, scriptwriting for sound, and new editing techniques. Although this transformation fully took hold in the 1930s, it began in our time frame, with Hollywood quickly becoming the "talkie capital" as well.

13. Economic Boom for the Region

Tourism Linked to Movies

Film fans across the country wanted to see the place where their favorite stars lived and worked. Tourism soared, with visitors flocking to Hollywood Boulevard, hoping for glimpses of filming or star sightings. Shops sold postcards, maps to the stars' homes, and souvenir photos. Some entrepreneurs launched bus tours, driving gawkers past celebrity mansions or studio gates. This synergy between tourism and film fed the city's economy.

Real Estate and Construction

The studios themselves required massive expansions. Sound stages, costume warehouses, and administrative offices rose on farmland or vacant lots. Laborers found jobs in construction, carpentry, painting, and electrical work. Meanwhile, new hotels, restaurants, and apartment buildings sprang up to house the influx of film workers. Hollywood's skyline changed as multi-story buildings replaced older, low structures. By the mid-1920s, the once-sleepy district looked like a bustling town of its own.

---

14. Critics and Detractors

Clash with Traditionalists

Some longtime Los Angeles residents viewed the film industry as a circus that brought loose morals, fast money, and scandal. They lamented that farmland was disappearing under studio lots and lavish star homes. Churches occasionally preached against Hollywood's influence, blaming it for rising divorce rates or rebellious youth. Local newspapers capitalized on star scandals—arrests for drunkenness, rumored affairs—sparking public debate about whether Hollywood was tarnishing the city's reputation.

Industry Growing Pains

Even inside the industry, not everyone welcomed the frantic pace. Overproduction sometimes led to low-quality films. Smaller studios went bankrupt amid competition from major players with bigger budgets. Labor disputes arose, as writers, set designers, and extras demanded fair pay. As with oil, the film boom was a rough frontier environment where fortunes were made and lost quickly.

15. Early Efforts at Preservation and Legacy

Collecting Film History

Some visionaries recognized that silent films were a new art form worth preserving. They kept copies of scripts, costumes, or still photographs. Archives were informally started by a few studios to store older film reels. However, the flammable nitrate film stock was a hazard, and fires occasionally destroyed valuable prints. True systematic preservation would come later, but seeds were planted to save a piece of Hollywood's story.

Hollywood Chamber of Commerce

In 1921, the **Hollywood Chamber of Commerce** formed, representing local businesses and seeking to improve the district's image. It promoted better roads, street lighting, and signs welcoming visitors. Over time, the chamber also supported publicity events like parades and festivals celebrating the industry's achievements. This organization worked closely with studios to coordinate marketing, establishing a pattern of mutual support that boosted both Hollywood's brand and local commerce.

---

16. The Hollywood Sign

A Real Estate Gimmick

Originally reading "HOLLYWOODLAND," the famous sign was erected in 1923 to advertise a new housing development in the hills above Hollywood. Each giant letter was 30 feet wide and 50 feet tall, illuminated by light bulbs. While it was meant to stand for just a year and a half, it became a cultural icon tied to the film industry's mystique. Over time, the "LAND" portion was removed, leaving the name "HOLLYWOOD" dominating the hillside.

17. Social Impact of Movie Stardom

Fan Clubs and Magazines

By the mid-1920s, fan clubs for stars like Rudolph Valentino, Clara Bow, or Harold Lloyd had chapters nationwide. Magazines such as **Photoplay** printed gossip, interviews, and behind-the-scenes photos, fueling an intense interest in celebrity lives. Fans wrote letters begging for autographed pictures or personal mementos. Publicists carefully curated star images, downplaying scandals and emphasizing romantic or comedic personas.

Shaping American Culture

Hollywood's silent films did not just entertain; they shaped national fashions, slang, and even attitudes. Audiences tried to mimic star mannerisms. New hairstyles or clothing lines were promoted as "just like in the pictures." This mass influence was unprecedented. The average American might never travel to Los Angeles, but they felt an intimate connection to Hollywood's glamour through the silver screen. This cultural power alarmed some moral guardians, who feared film's ability to transform public opinion.

18. The Growing Power of Studio Moguls

Notable Figures

Men like **Adolph Zukor** (Paramount), **William Fox** (Fox Film Corporation), **Louis B. Mayer** (who would form Metro-Goldwyn-Mayer), and the **Warner Brothers** built empires that dominated the film industry. They negotiated star contracts, financed expensive productions, and decided which scripts got made. Nicknamed "studio moguls," these executives often began as immigrants or small-time entrepreneurs and rose to immense wealth. Their decisions could create or break careers overnight.

Consolidation and Competition

While the major studios worked together on distribution and some censorship matters, they also competed fiercely for big stars and lucrative stories. Each aimed to produce prestige films that won critical praise while maintaining a steady output of genre pictures—westerns, comedies, romances—to keep theaters busy. By 1929, a handful of studios controlled most of Hollywood's output, a system that would endure well into the mid-20th century.

---

19. The End of the Silent Era and Beyond

Transition to Sound

As the 1920s ended, silent films gave way to "talkies." This shift was both thrilling and disruptive. Many silent stars struggled with microphones, poor diction, or heavy accents. Some adapted successfully, like Mary Pickford, who won an Oscar for a talkie performance. Others, like John Gilbert, saw their careers stall. Meanwhile, new stars emerged, chosen for clear voices and strong screen presence. Studios spent fortunes building sound stages, equipping theaters with audio systems, and training crews in the art of sound recording.

Setting the Stage for the Future

As the 1920s turned into the 1930s, Hollywood had become a household name worldwide. Los Angeles was now tied in the public mind to motion pictures, sunshine, and star-studded glamour—despite the city's continued reliance on oil, manufacturing, and real estate. The next major challenge for the film industry would be the **Great Depression**, which tested the studios' financial might and forced them to adapt storylines for a nation in crisis.

CHAPTER 17

The Great Depression and Rebuilding

By the late 1920s, Los Angeles was booming. Hollywood films were popular around the world, oil wells fueled a strong economy, and the city kept expanding outward. But no place was immune to the country's biggest economic crisis: the **Great Depression**, triggered by the stock market crash of 1929. In this chapter, we will see how Los Angeles felt the Depression, including the rise in unemployment, the dust bowl migrants, and the public works projects that reshaped parts of the city. We will also learn how local leadership tried to steer the city through hard times, setting the stage for a slow but steady recovery that would eventually lead into new opportunities in the 1940s.

1. The Crash of 1929 and Its Immediate Effects

Optimism Turns to Fear

Throughout most of the 1920s, many Angelenos believed the good times would never end. Oil production was strong, Hollywood was thriving, and real estate values often climbed. But when the stock market collapsed in October 1929, confidence across the nation quickly eroded. While the collapse was centered on Wall Street in New York, its effects rippled across the country. People who had invested in stocks, including some in Los Angeles, lost large sums. Banks began to fail, or they limited credit, which hurt businesses needing loans.

Initial Denial in Los Angeles

At first, many in Los Angeles thought the downturn would be brief. The city had a more diversified economy—oil, films, manufacturing, and agriculture—so some leaders hoped these industries would cushion the blow. For a short while, local newspapers insisted that Southern California was "recession-proof." However, as 1930 wore on, production slowed, people lost jobs, and it became clear Los Angeles would not escape the nationwide slump.

2. Unemployment and Hardship

Job Losses Across Industries

By 1931 and 1932, factories began laying off workers due to reduced demand for cars, steel products, and consumer goods. Oil companies cut back on drilling new wells, focusing on maintaining existing production. Film studios also decreased output. While Hollywood remained a popular form of entertainment, many studios trimmed budgets and staff, especially for lower-priority projects. These job cuts spread, creating a ripple effect in service sectors like retail, restaurants, and transportation.

Migrant Workers and Housing Crises

Los Angeles also faced a major influx of migrants from other parts of the country—especially the Midwest and Southwest regions battered by the Dust Bowl. These newcomers arrived seeking agricultural or urban work. Many settled in shantytowns (sometimes called "Hoovervilles") along riverbeds or vacant lots, living in tents, wooden shacks, or cardboard shelters. Local charities and churches tried to offer food and blankets, but resources were limited. The city government struggled to cope with these growing informal settlements.

---

3. The Dust Bowl and Okie Migration

Worsening Farm Conditions Elsewhere

Starting in the early 1930s, droughts in states like Oklahoma, Texas, Kansas, and Arkansas turned farmland into dry, dusty plains. Massive dust storms blew away topsoil, making it impossible for many farmers to stay afloat. Forced to abandon their homes, they loaded up cars or trucks and headed west, drawn by rumors that California—particularly the Los Angeles area—still had jobs and fertile farmland.

Reality on Arrival

Many of these "Okies" (a nickname often used for migrants from Oklahoma, though it was applied broadly) discovered that work was scarce. Large farms in California favored seasonal or migrant labor, paying very low wages. Competition was fierce, and living conditions were harsh. In Los Angeles, many found only part-time factory or construction jobs, if at all. They set up camps on the edges of the city, hoping times would improve. These camps could be unsanitary and vulnerable to floods or disease outbreaks.

---

4. Public Response and Local Charity

City and County Relief

Los Angeles County established some relief agencies to provide food or small cash payments to unemployed families. But limited budgets and rising need meant many were turned away or received only minimal help. Local officials argued about whether it was the city's role or the state's role to fund large-scale relief. Meanwhile, lines at soup kitchens and relief offices grew longer. Some unemployed men sold apples or shined shoes on street corners, while women took in laundry or performed domestic work to keep their families fed.

Churches and Philanthropists

Religious groups—Catholic missions, Protestant churches, and Jewish charities—stepped in to offer hot meals, clothing drives, or shelter beds. Civic clubs like the Rotary and Kiwanis organized soup kitchens or distributed blankets. A few wealthy individuals contributed funds for emergency relief. Hollywood celebrities occasionally did charity events, donating proceeds to the poor. Though these efforts helped, they could not solve the deeper economic crisis. Angelenos had to wait for federal programs to arrive.

5. Federal Programs under the New Deal

Franklin D. Roosevelt's Election

In 1933, Franklin D. Roosevelt became President, promising a "New Deal" to combat the Depression. The federal government launched agencies like the **Works Progress Administration (WPA)**, **Civilian Conservation Corps (CCC)**, and the **Public Works Administration (PWA)**. These aimed to create jobs, build infrastructure, and restore public confidence. Los Angeles quickly applied for funds to construct roads, public buildings, and other improvements.

Local Projects

Under the WPA, Angelenos worked on tasks such as paving streets, building sidewalks, improving schools, and painting murals in public buildings. The PWA funded larger projects like waterworks, bridges, and expansions to ports. The CCC placed young men in conservation camps in nearby forests or parks, teaching them skills while they planted trees or built trails. These projects provided much-needed paychecks, though wages were modest. They also improved the city's infrastructure for future growth.

---

6. Construction of Civic Landmarks

Union Station

One of the most famous Depression-era projects in Los Angeles was **Union Station**, completed in 1939. It brought together multiple rail lines—previously scattered—into one grand terminal near downtown. The architecture combined Spanish Colonial, Mission Revival, and Art Deco touches, symbolizing the city's cultural heritage. Construction employed hundreds of workers, which was a major boost during hard times. When it opened, Union Station stood as a proud statement of Los Angeles' importance as a transportation hub.

Griffith Observatory

Though planning began earlier, the **Griffith Observatory** was constructed and opened in 1935, aided by city and philanthropic funds. Named after

Griffith J. Griffith, who donated the land, it provided Angelenos a public observatory and planetarium. Workers built roads, landscaped the grounds, and erected the structure. The observatory became a source of civic pride, offering educational programs even when the economy struggled.

7. The Film Industry Adapts

Escapist Movies

While unemployment soared, film-going remained a popular pastime. People wanted distraction from daily worries, so Hollywood studios produced musicals, comedies, and adventure films that gave audiences hope or laughter. Classics like "42nd Street" and the early "Shirley Temple" features lifted spirits. Meanwhile, the new sound technology that arrived in the late 1920s matured, and "talkies" dominated screens by the mid-1930s.

Studio Consolidation

The Depression forced some smaller studios to merge or close. Major players—MGM, Paramount, Warner Bros., 20th Century-Fox, and RKO—tightened budgets but held onto their theater chains. They perfected the **studio system**, controlling star rosters and distribution. Government scrutiny arose about monopolistic practices, but the nation's bigger concern was economic recovery. In Los Angeles, film production kept employing a sizable workforce of actors, directors, technicians, and extras. This steadied part of the local economy compared to regions that lacked a robust entertainment sector.

8. Oil Production and Price Slumps

Overproduction and Low Prices

During the Depression, the oil sector faced low prices as demand dropped. Factories used less fuel, and families cut back on driving. California's oil fields produced more crude than markets could absorb, pushing prices down. Some wells shut, and drilling almost halted. Major oil companies tried to reduce output to stabilize prices, but smaller operators often kept pumping to make any profit they could. This chaotic approach meant many lost money, while the environment suffered from neglected or abandoned wells.

Impacts on Workers

Thousands of oil-field workers lost their jobs, adding to unemployment. Fields that once had bustling camps became ghostly. Some rig hands sought other work with WPA projects or returned to farming if they could. Unions made small inroads, attempting to secure minimum wages, but with so many unemployed, companies had the upper hand. In Los Angeles, some petroleum refining continued, but expansion paused until the economy improved later in the 1930s.

9. Agriculture in Crisis

Falling Crop Prices

Although Los Angeles was increasingly urban, the surrounding counties still relied on agriculture—citrus, vegetables, and dairy. The Depression hammered crop prices, leaving farmers with surplus produce they could not sell at profitable rates. Some fruit rotted in orchards because transporting and selling it cost more than the market price. Government programs bought or destroyed surpluses to stabilize prices, an approach that angered hungry people who saw good food wasted.

Migrant Labor Issues

Migrant laborers, including Dust Bowl refugees, continued to flow into the region. Growers welcomed cheap labor but paid extremely low wages. Strikes and protests erupted in agricultural communities around Los Angeles, sometimes meeting violent crackdowns from local authorities. Labor organizers sought better conditions, but public sympathy was mixed.

Many city residents blamed migrants for job competition, while others realized these people were fleeing desperate conditions and needed fair treatment.

10. Rise of Politicians and Populist Ideas

Upton Sinclair and EPIC

One notable political figure during this era was **Upton Sinclair**, a socialist writer famous for "The Jungle." In 1934, he ran for governor of California under the banner of the **EPIC** movement—"End Poverty in California." Sinclair proposed cooperative factories and land colonies for the unemployed. His candidacy inspired hope among many poor and working-class Angelenos, but wealthy interests and Hollywood studio heads opposed him, fearing radical changes. He lost the election, highlighting a deep divide in California politics between reformers and conservative business leaders.

Local Government Shifts

In Los Angeles, mayors and council members faced growing pressure to expand relief programs. Some proposed municipal ownership of utilities or more extensive public works. Others insisted on conservative budgets to avoid city debt. Meanwhile, individuals like **Frank L. Shaw** served as mayor (1933–1938), backing some New Deal projects while trying to keep city finances under control. Corruption scandals also shook City Hall, reflecting tensions over how to handle relief funds and job placements.

11. Social and Cultural Shifts

Impact on Families

With incomes reduced, families often doubled up in small apartments or single homes. Young adults delayed marriage or children for financial reasons. Some children left school early to help earn money, although child labor laws offered limited protection. The emotional toll of joblessness was high. Breadwinners felt shame at not providing for loved ones, and mental health problems rose, though formal support systems were scarce.

Racial Segregation

Racial minorities, already facing housing and job discrimination, endured deeper hardships. African Americans found themselves at the bottom of hiring lists, forced into the toughest, lowest-paying tasks. Mexican Americans, both U.S.-born and immigrants, confronted deportation campaigns by local authorities who saw them as "taking American jobs." These deportations, sometimes called "repatriation," uprooted thousands who had lived in Los Angeles for years. Asian Americans, especially Japanese and Chinese communities, also faced job discrimination and hostility from those blaming them for economic woes.

---

12. Cultural Expressions of the Depression

Art and Murals

Inspired by Mexican muralists like Diego Rivera, local artists painted large public murals depicting workers, farmers, and social themes. Under the WPA's Federal Art Project, murals adorned schools, libraries, and community centers. They celebrated cooperation, labor, and the city's diverse heritage. Painters and sculptors who had struggled to sell their art found a modest income through these federal programs, leaving behind a lasting cultural legacy.

Music and Theater

Folk music events, union protest songs, and community theater productions blossomed. The Federal Theatre Project sponsored plays, giving work to actors and stagehands. These productions often tackled social issues, from unemployment to workers' rights, sparking conversations among audiences about the nation's direction. Neighborhood gatherings for free concerts or performances offered a morale boost, proving that creativity endured despite poverty.

13. Rebuilding Infrastructure

Massive Flood Control Projects

Los Angeles learned harsh lessons from recurring floods in the 1910s and 1920s. The Los Angeles River and smaller waterways often overflowed during heavy rains, damaging homes and farmland. During the Depression, the city secured federal funds to channelize the river, constructing **concrete flood control channels**. By the late 1930s, much of the river was lined with concrete, altering its natural course but protecting growing neighborhoods from destructive floods. Critics lamented the loss of a living waterway, but city planners saw it as necessary for safety and development.

Expanding Roads and Bridges

New Deal money also helped upgrade roads to accommodate increasing car ownership. Crews built or widened major boulevards, adding better paving. Bridges crossing the Los Angeles River and other channels were replaced with sturdy structures—some with Art Deco designs. Although the city still had a strong streetcar network, these improved roads hinted at a future oriented toward automobiles, a shift that would accelerate in coming decades.

---

14. Community Organizing and Labor Unions

Growing Union Movements

Fed up with dire conditions, more workers turned to labor unions. The **Congress of Industrial Organizations (CIO)** gained ground among factory and service workers. Film industry unions—like the Screen Actors Guild (founded in 1933)—emerged to protect stars and technicians alike. Though studios and big businesses resisted unionization, the New Deal's pro-labor stance made it somewhat easier for workers to organize. Strikes and negotiations led to modest wage gains, workplace safety rules, and job security measures.

Tenant and Neighborhood Groups

In poor areas, neighbors formed tenant associations to fight evictions or rent hikes. Communities of color organized mutual-aid societies to share food, clothing, or job leads. Such grassroots activism connected people who felt overlooked by city or state officials. Although resources were slim, solidarity gave them a voice in local politics. When entire neighborhoods faced eviction, these groups sometimes staged protests or blockades, drawing public attention to their plight.

15. Sports and Entertainment Diversify

Baseball and Other Sports

During tough times, people still craved affordable recreation. Local baseball teams—both professional and semi-pro—continued to draw crowds. The Pacific Coast League had a strong following in Los Angeles, with teams like the Los Angeles Angels and Hollywood Stars. Boxing matches remained popular, often held in open arenas or small venues. These sports events offered a temporary escape, with cheap tickets and lively atmospheres.

Radio's Golden Age

Radio ownership soared in the 1930s, providing free entertainment in living rooms. Angelenos listened to comedy shows, dramas, and news broadcasts from local stations or nationwide networks. Sponsors found radio an effective advertising platform, so even with the Depression, certain radio personalities earned good salaries. Local radio theaters sometimes staged live broadcasts with audiences, further enriching the city's cultural landscape.

16. Tourism During Hard Times

Decline Then Small Recovery

Overall tourism dipped early in the Depression, as fewer Americans had money for travel. Many hotels in downtown Los Angeles and beach areas saw occupancy drop. Some resorts and attractions struggled to stay open. However, by the mid-1930s, modest improvements arrived. Visitors still found the region's climate appealing, and with cheap gasoline, some families drove west for a budget vacation. The presence of Hollywood also continued to lure curious fans hoping to spot a star.

Promotional Campaigns

City promoters tried to maintain Los Angeles' image as a sunny paradise. Chambers of commerce distributed pamphlets touting year-round mild weather and scenic beauty. Travel articles showed pictures of palm-lined streets, ignoring the shantytowns. While critics called this a whitewashing of reality, tourism dollars did help certain businesses survive. Hotels, restaurants, and souvenir shops adapted by offering discounted packages and simpler meals to attract price-conscious travelers.

---

17. Shantytowns and Homelessness

Hoovervilles in Los Angeles

As unemployment soared, homeless encampments mushroomed. People built makeshift shelters from scrap wood, metal, or cardboard, often near the Los Angeles River or vacant industrial land. These "Hoovervilles" (named mockingly after President Herbert Hoover) were rarely sanctioned. City health officials worried about disease, while police sometimes raided camps, evicting residents. But more sprang up elsewhere, a sad testament to the depth of the economic crisis.

Conflicts and Evictions

Property owners demanded the city remove these encampments to prevent land devaluation. Some local politicians argued that forcing these camps out might push people to find better shelter or leave the area, but there were few alternatives. Temporary relief programs housed some in converted armories or government buildings, but capacity was limited. The result was an ongoing cycle of displacement, with families repeatedly uprooted. This fueled resentment toward local authorities seen as ignoring the poor.

18. Steps Toward Recovery in the Late 1930s

Gradual Improvement

By 1935–1936, signs of economic stabilization appeared nationwide, including in Los Angeles. New Deal spending injected cash into construction, roads, and public welfare. Some industries like film slowly rebounded, producing hits that drew large audiences. Even the oil sector recovered a bit as factories again needed fuel. Although unemployment remained high, the trend was upward, and fewer people lived in absolute crisis.

Political Changes

Angelenos began electing leaders more open to social reforms. In 1938, **Culbert L. Olson**, a Democrat, became governor of California, reflecting shifting political attitudes. In the city, officials moved to coordinate better housing and job creation. Local labor unions had greater influence, pressing for fair wages and improved conditions. By the end of the decade, Los Angeles was not fully prosperous, but the dire emergency of 1932–1933 had eased.

19. Cultural Milestones

The 1932 Summer Olympics

In 1932, Los Angeles hosted the Summer Olympic Games—an event planned before the Depression. Despite economic struggles, the city completed the main stadium (the Los Angeles Memorial Coliseum) and athletes' facilities. Many nations participated, though some sent smaller teams due to travel costs. The Games boosted city morale, showing the world that Los Angeles could host a major international event. While attendance was lower than hoped, the spectacle was a welcome break from daily worries.

Hollywood's Bright Spot

Hollywood responded to the Depression with elaborate musicals like "42nd Street" (1933) and "Top Hat" (1935), plus comedies, gangster films, and monster classics from Universal Studios. Stars like Clark Gable, Jean Harlow, and Shirley Temple entertained millions, offering escapism. Disney's "Snow White and the Seven Dwarfs" (1937) became a massive hit. These successes meant the film industry, though not recession-proof, provided a glimmer of financial stability and hope.

CHAPTER 18

World War II and Post-War Shifts

The late 1930s brought hints of recovery in Los Angeles, but it was the outbreak of **World War II** that truly revitalized the region's economy. Defense contracts poured in, new factories opened, and tens of thousands of workers arrived from all over the country to take part in the war effort. In this chapter, we will see how Los Angeles turned into a major hub for aircraft and shipbuilding, how the war affected local communities, and how the city changed again once the fighting ended. Though we are focusing on older times, the 1940s stand as a crucial turning point when Los Angeles' population and industries exploded, setting the foundation for the metropolis we know today.

1. Prelude to War and Defense Contracts

Rising International Tensions

By the late 1930s, tensions were mounting in Europe and Asia. Germany's expansion under Hitler and Japan's militarism signaled looming conflict. The United States remained officially neutral but began rearming. Factories that had been slow during the Depression now saw a surge in government orders for planes, tanks, and ships. Los Angeles, with its mild climate and open land, was a prime spot for building large military production facilities.

Government Spending

Even before the U.S. entered the war, the federal government offered contracts to companies that could supply arms to allies. Aircraft manufacturing, which had a small presence in Southern California, blossomed. Firms like **Lockheed**, **Douglas**, and **North American Aviation** expanded factories near Los Angeles. They hired engineers and assembly-line workers, many trained in New Deal vocational programs. This ramp-up, known as the "Arsenal of Democracy," revived struggling communities and laid the groundwork for wartime production.

2. The Attack on Pearl Harbor and Mobilization

December 7, 1941

Everything changed when Japan attacked Pearl Harbor in Hawaii on December 7, 1941. The next day, the United States declared war on Japan, soon followed by declarations against Germany and Italy. Across the nation, industries pivoted to full-scale war production. In Los Angeles, factories switched from consumer goods to military hardware seemingly overnight. Automobile plants produced trucks for the Army, and machine shops churned out bullets or airplane parts.

Fear of West Coast Invasion

Because Hawaii and parts of the Pacific had been targeted, many Angelenos worried that Southern California could be next. Blackouts were enforced at night to hide city lights from potential enemy planes. Anti-aircraft guns were placed on rooftops, and civilian defense groups trained to respond to bombing raids. Though an actual invasion never occurred, the sense of urgency spurred fast construction of more defense plants and airfields.

---

3. Aircraft Industry Boom

Major Companies

Before WWII, local aircraft firms included **Lockheed** in Burbank and **Douglas** in Santa Monica. With war orders, these and newer companies expanded drastically. They built sprawling plants with assembly lines that could produce hundreds of planes each month, from fighters like the P-38 Lightning (Lockheed) to bombers like the A-20 (Douglas). Skilled machinists, engineers, and draftsmen flooded the region to help design new models.

Rosie the Riveter and Women Workers

As men joined the military, factories needed more labor. Women stepped in, symbolized by the "Rosie the Riveter" icon. In Los Angeles, women learned to rivet aircraft panels, wire electronics, and test engines. They wore coveralls and safety gear, breaking stereotypes about women's roles in heavy industry. Though not always paid the same as men, they gained independence and pride in supporting the war effort. After the war, many faced layoffs or pressure to return to traditional roles, but the experience planted seeds of greater gender equality in the workplace.

---

4. Shipbuilding and the Port of Los Angeles

Wartime Shipyards

Along the coast, existing shipyards in **San Pedro** and **Wilmington** greatly expanded. New yards were built to produce cargo ships (Liberty ships), warships, and troop transports. The war demanded a huge fleet to supply U.S. forces worldwide, so thousands of welders, pipefitters, and steelworkers toiled around the clock. Shipbuilding offered good wages, drawing workers from rural areas and distant states. The port's growth outpaced any previous era, turning it into a bustling center of maritime activity.

Housing Pressures

With so many newcomers, housing shortages reached crisis levels. Families packed into small apartments near the harbor, and temporary housing sprang up for shipyard employees. The federal government funded some housing projects, but demand far exceeded supply. Long lines formed for rentals, and overcrowding led to sanitation problems. This shortage was repeated around aircraft plants as well, pushing Los Angeles to its limits.

---

5. Demographic Changes

Wartime Migration

The war brought a large influx of people seeking defense jobs. States like Texas, Arkansas, and Louisiana—still struggling economically—sent thousands of workers west. African Americans, barred from many Southern jobs by segregation, found better opportunities in Los Angeles factories, though they still faced discrimination in housing and promotions. This migration diversified the city further, adding to existing communities of color.

Tensions and Racial Conflict

Not all welcomed these changes. White residents sometimes resisted integrated neighborhoods, forming associations to uphold restrictive covenants that barred minorities from certain areas. Friction mounted as more African American families tried to settle in historically white zones. Meanwhile, Latino workers faced similar struggles. The most dramatic incident was the **Zoot Suit Riots** of 1943, where white servicemen clashed with young Mexican Americans (pachucos) wearing zoot suits, revealing deep racial tensions beneath the city's defense-fueled prosperity.

6. The Zoot Suit Riots and Social Unrest

Causes and Context

Los Angeles had seen tensions over jobs, housing, and cultural differences. Young Mexican American men wearing zoot suits—long jackets, baggy pants, and flashy accessories—were often stereotyped as gang members or troublemakers. When a group of sailors claimed they were attacked by zoot-suiters, media coverage fanned anti-Mexican sentiment. Military personnel roamed downtown and East Los Angeles, assaulting anyone in zoot suits, tearing off clothes, and beating them.

City Response

The police often arrested the victims rather than the attackers, which outraged the Mexican American community. Newspapers printed sensational headlines. Officials eventually quelled the riots, but the damage was done. The event highlighted racial inequalities. Although the war effort preached unity against a foreign enemy, at home, prejudice still flourished. Calls for improved community relations grew, but real progress was slow.

7. Japanese American Internment

Executive Order 9066

One of the darkest episodes of WWII on the West Coast was the **internment of Japanese Americans**. After Pearl Harbor, fear and suspicion of anyone of Japanese ancestry soared. In early 1942, President Roosevelt signed Executive Order 9066, allowing military authorities to remove people from designated "military areas." On the West Coast, this meant forcing Japanese Americans—citizens and non-citizens alike—to leave their homes and report to "relocation centers."

Effects in Los Angeles

Japanese American neighborhoods like Little Tokyo were emptied as families hurriedly sold or stored their belongings, often at huge losses. They were sent to camps in remote areas such as Manzanar, in California's Owens Valley, living behind barbed wire for much of the war. Businesses that Japanese Americans had built over generations were lost or taken by opportunists. The policy caused deep trauma and a legacy of distrust. After the war, some returned to Los Angeles, finding their homes or shops gone. Rebuilding took years, and the hurt lingered for decades.

---

8. Women on the Home Front

Broader Roles

Beyond aircraft riveters, women also took on roles in offices, government agencies, hospitals, and civil defense. They organized scrap drives for metal, rubber, and other materials needed by factories. Female volunteers joined organizations like the Red Cross or USO (United Service Organizations), supporting troops with care packages or entertainment. Women's presence in the workforce increased acceptance of their capabilities, although sexist attitudes persisted.

Daycare and Family Changes

With both parents working, families needed childcare options. Some factories offered on-site daycare or partnered with community centers.

This was a first step toward acknowledging that women's labor was essential. Wartime separation also affected marriages—many wives stayed in Los Angeles while husbands served overseas. Letters and ration books, rather than shared daily life, were the norm. After the war, returning veterans and working women often negotiated new family dynamics.

---

9. Wartime Rationing and Daily Life

Ration Coupons

Gasoline, meat, sugar, tires, and other items were rationed to support the war effort. Angelenos received coupon books limiting how much they could buy each month. People formed carpool clubs to save gas, or they used public transport more often. Victory gardens sprang up in backyards, growing vegetables to supplement rationed food. Though some chafed at these limits, most recognized the need and took pride in "doing their part."

Blackouts and Civil Defense

Coastal cities like Los Angeles enforced nighttime blackouts to make it harder for potential enemy bombers or submarines to spot targets. Residents used blackout curtains, and streetlights were dimmed. Air-raid wardens patrolled neighborhoods, ensuring compliance. Sirens were tested regularly. While no major attack happened on Los Angeles, occasional false alarms, like the "Battle of Los Angeles" in 1942, caused panic. These experiences shaped a generation that lived with the constant awareness of global conflict.

---

10. Economic Boom Despite Hardships

Surge in Employment

By 1943–1944, war production had slashed unemployment to near zero. Factories ran multiple shifts, paying wages above pre-war levels. Many families saved money for the first time, though rationing limited what they could buy. A sense of prosperity returned, at least for those employed in defense work. This starkly contrasted with the Depression years, although not everyone benefited equally—racial discrimination in hiring was still prevalent.

Federal Investment

Los Angeles benefited from huge federal spending on military bases, shipyards, and airfields. This included expansions at places like **March Field** (an Army Air Corps base) and new training sites around the region. Military contracts also spurred infrastructure improvements—better roads to transport tanks and planes, expanded ports for shipping. All of this set the stage for post-war growth when these facilities converted to peacetime uses or supported new industries.

11. Servicemen's Experiences

Local Enlistment and Deployment

Thousands of Los Angeles men joined the armed forces, serving in Europe, North Africa, and the Pacific. Women also enlisted in groups like the Women's Army Corps (WAC) or WAVES (Navy). Letters home described battles far away, while local radio and newspapers tracked the progress of divisions containing Angelenos. Neighborhoods displayed "blue star" flags in windows to honor family members in service, and gold stars if a loved one was killed in action.

Returning Veterans

By 1945, as victory approached, soldiers began returning. They brought experiences of seeing the world, forging new friendships across racial or regional lines. Many used the G.I. Bill, which provided low-interest home loans and college funding. This program would soon transform Los Angeles neighborhoods, fueling housing construction and higher education enrollment. But first, the city had to transition from a war footing to peacetime.

12. Racial Integration Movements

Pressure for Civil Rights

Black Americans and other minorities who served or worked in war industries felt they had proven their loyalty and capabilities. They expected better treatment after the war, including fair housing, integrated neighborhoods, and equal job opportunities. Civil rights groups grew stronger, pointing to war rhetoric about "freedom" and "democracy" that should apply at home. Instances of housing discrimination or workplace segregation drew protests and legal challenges.

The Sleepy Lagoon Case and Aftermath

During the war, the **Sleepy Lagoon** murder case in 1942 saw a group of Mexican American youths wrongly convicted of murder with little evidence, amid anti-Mexican sentiment. Civil rights activists fought to overturn the convictions. Their eventual success in 1944 was a landmark for challenging biased policing and courts. This case, along with the Zoot Suit Riots, highlighted the city's need to address prejudice. After the war, more attention was paid to bridging racial divides, though progress was slow.

---

13. War's End and the Immediate Aftermath

V-E and V-J Days

When Germany surrendered in May 1945 (V-E Day) and Japan surrendered in August 1945 (V-J Day), Los Angeles erupted in celebration. Sailors and factory workers flooded downtown streets, cheering, dancing, and hugging strangers. People tore ration books or burned blackout curtains in jubilation. Factories began to pivot back to civilian goods. Over the next year, millions of servicemen poured home, reuniting families and straining the city's infrastructure once again.

Conversion to Peacetime Production

With the war over, defense orders dropped sharply. Some factories closed or laid off workers, leading to short-term unemployment spikes. But overall, Los Angeles' newly skilled workforce found ways to adapt. Aviation companies turned to commercial airliners. Shipyards repaired existing fleets or built passenger vessels. Electronics, plastics, and automobile industries also grew, benefiting from wartime research and manufacturing techniques.

14. Housing Crisis and Suburban Growth

The GI Bill and Home Loans

Returning veterans took advantage of government-backed mortgages to buy homes. Demand skyrocketed, but Los Angeles had not built enough housing during the war. Developers raced to create suburban tracts in places like the **San Fernando Valley** and Orange County. Simple, single-story "starter homes" sprang up by the thousands. Roads, schools, and shopping centers followed. This "suburban boom" would dominate the next decades, though it began in the late 1940s.

Levittowns and Local Equivalents

While the famous Levittown developments were on the East Coast, similar concepts appeared in Southern California: uniform houses on curving streets, designed for quick construction. Local builders refined techniques like mass-produced frames and standardized floor plans. Although these suburbs offered a dream of homeownership, they often used restrictive covenants or unwritten rules to exclude minority buyers. This shaped Los Angeles' racial geography for years to come.

15. Shifts in Transportation

The Slow Decline of Streetcars

During WWII, streetcars had remained vital, transporting defense workers. But car ownership soared after the war, aided by cheap gas and returning soldiers eager for personal vehicles. Oil companies, car manufacturers, and developers advocated for highways over rail. Funding for streetcar maintenance lagged. By the late 1940s, private operators of the **Pacific Electric** and **Los Angeles Railway** found profits dwindling. The stage was set for eventual dismantling of the streetcar system in favor of buses and freeways.

Freeway Beginnings

Los Angeles had begun planning freeways before the war, but construction was slow. Now, with federal aid and the impetus of returning GIs, the city laid out grand designs for multiple freeways linking downtown to suburbs. The first major stretch, the **Arroyo Seco Parkway** (later Pasadena Freeway), had opened in 1940, but post-war expansions in the late 1940s and beyond would define the region's car-centric future. Initially, Angelenos marveled at these modern roadways, seeing them as symbols of progress.

16. Hollywood's Transition to Post-War

Wartime Propaganda Films

Hollywood studios had produced patriotic films and training reels during the war. Documentaries, musicals with wartime themes, and dramas about heroism reflected the conflict. With peace restored, audiences desired new stories. War films continued but shifted focus to veterans' experiences or spy thrillers set in post-war Europe. Meanwhile, film noir—dark crime stories—became popular, reflecting a more cynical mood after the global turmoil.

Labor Strikes and Television

Shortly after WWII, Hollywood faced labor unrest. Unions representing actors, writers, and technicians demanded better pay and residuals. Strikes occasionally shut down studios. Another threat was **television**, emerging in the late 1940s. Although still limited, it promised in-home entertainment that could rival the cinema. Studios scrambled to adapt, investing in color film, widescreen formats, and lavish spectacles to keep audiences in theaters. Los Angeles, as the home of both film and soon TV, braced for changes ahead.

17. Changing Racial Landscapes

African American Migration Continues

During and after the war, more African Americans arrived, drawn by defense or factory jobs. They settled in neighborhoods like Watts, South Central, and parts of Compton, areas often restricted by real estate practices. This population growth established vibrant churches, music scenes (jazz, R&B), and community organizations. Despite ongoing discrimination, these communities laid strong roots, influencing city culture in lasting ways.

Mexican American Identity

Mexican Americans, who had contributed to the war effort at home and abroad, hoped for improved status. Some veterans used the GI Bill to attend college, stepping into professional roles. However, housing discrimination and low-wage labor remained a barrier for many families. The activism sparked by the Zoot Suit Riots continued, with civil rights leaders pushing for integrated schools and fair housing. Bit by bit, local politics responded, though progress was uneven.

18. Economic Trends and Labor Challenges

Post-War Recession Fears

As the war ended, some economists predicted a new depression if defense spending disappeared. But massive consumer demand for cars, appliances, and homes spurred the economy instead. Factories retooled for civilian products—planes for commercial airlines, electronics for household use, and so on. Los Angeles thrived as a hub of new technology, with engineers and scientists staying from war projects.

Worker Adjustments

Many women who had entered factories during the war were pushed out when male veterans returned. Some remained by choice or necessity, but cultural norms nudged others back to traditional domestic roles. African American and Mexican American workers faced last-hired, first-fired patterns. Unions fought for seniority rights, but management sometimes resisted. Overall, wartime experiences had broadened many people's horizons, planting seeds for future civil rights and feminist movements.

19. The Cold War Emerges

Military-Industrial Complex

As WWII concluded, tensions with the Soviet Union escalated, marking the start of the **Cold War**. For Los Angeles, this meant continued demand for aerospace and defense research. The city's aircraft companies shifted to jet technology, missiles, and space exploration concepts. Secret labs and defense contractors multiplied around the region, ensuring that even after WWII, the defense sector would remain crucial. This shaped the local economy well into later decades, though we focus here on its early post-war formation.

Civil Defense Preparedness

Fearing a nuclear conflict, city officials promoted civil defense drills, air-raid sirens, and designated fallout shelters. Schoolchildren practiced "duck and cover" drills. While no nuclear attack happened, this era's anxieties influenced architecture (with minimal windows or bomb-shelter basements) and public planning. Los Angeles, once worried about Japanese bombers, now fretted over Soviet missiles.

CHAPTER 19

Mid-Century Development

By the end of World War II, Los Angeles was already one of the biggest, busiest cities in the United States. The 1950s and early 1960s brought even more change, as returning veterans used the G.I. Bill to buy homes in newly built suburbs, families acquired multiple cars, and the booming aerospace and entertainment industries kept money and people flowing into Southern California. In this chapter, we will explore how the city navigated this period of massive suburban expansion, the construction of freeways, cultural shifts, growing racial tensions, and environmental concerns. We will see how mid-century Los Angeles took steps toward the region we can recognize, even as it still clung to older patterns and faced the challenges that come with rapid, sprawling development.

1. Suburban Explosion

The Post-War Housing Boom

With World War II over, returning soldiers and their families needed places to live. Under the **G.I. Bill**, veterans could secure low-interest loans, spurring a huge wave of home buying. Developers in the Los Angeles region quickly turned farmland and open space into vast tracts of affordable houses. Unlike the pre-war era, these houses often came with modern amenities: attached garages, lawns, and brand-new appliances. Construction methods improved, using assembly-line techniques to build entire neighborhoods rapidly.

Subdivisions spread into areas like the **San Fernando Valley**, the eastern stretches of Los Angeles County, and Orange County to the south. The typical layout featured curving streets, cul-de-sacs, and standardized floor plans—an updated version of earlier building booms, but on a much larger scale. Such uniform neighborhoods reflected the ideal of the "American Dream": a single-family home with a yard, made accessible to many thanks to G.I. Bill financing.

Growing Pains

However, the rapid suburbanization overwhelmed existing infrastructure. Schools, roads, and utilities sometimes lagged behind the influx of new residents. Temporary classrooms and hastily installed sewer lines strained local budgets. Meanwhile, farmland vanished at an astonishing rate, causing concern among those who still valued agriculture. But for most, the promise of a roomy house and wide streets symbolized progress, especially compared to cramped city apartments or older neighborhoods left behind by freeway routes.

---

2. The Age of Freeways

From Streetcars to Highways

In earlier decades, Los Angeles had boasted one of the world's largest electric streetcar networks, the **Pacific Electric** Red Cars and the Los Angeles Railway Yellow Cars. But by the late 1940s, private car ownership surged. Oil, tire, and automotive interests encouraged this shift, and public policy backed them up. Officials believed freeways were the best way to handle the city's future traffic needs, so they planned a vast system of wide, high-speed roads linking downtown to outlying suburbs.

In the 1950s, the construction of major freeways accelerated: the **Harbor Freeway**, **Hollywood Freeway**, and parts of the **Santa Ana Freeway** opened, among others. Early on, these roads were admired for their modern design, artful overpasses, and well-landscaped medians. Public relations campaigns promoted freeways as symbols of prosperity and convenience, offering families quick access to jobs and shopping centers—assuming they could afford a car.

Displacement and Community Impacts

Building freeways often cut through older, lower-income neighborhoods, displacing residents and businesses with limited compensation. In East Los Angeles, Boyle Heights, and parts of South Central, entire blocks were demolished to clear right-of-ways. Many of those affected were African American, Mexican American, or working-class white families without the political power to protect their homes. This led to enduring resentment. Some communities became isolated by towering concrete walls and interchanges, losing walkability and local cohesion. Freeways thus shaped not just transportation, but the city's social and racial landscape for decades.

3. Redlining and Housing Segregation

Restrictive Covenants

During this mid-century housing boom, not everyone had equal access. Real estate practices known as **redlining** labeled certain areas as "high risk" for loans—often based on racial demographics. Meanwhile, **restrictive covenants** on property deeds explicitly forbade selling homes to non-white buyers. Though the Supreme Court ruled these covenants unenforceable in 1948 (Shelley v. Kraemer), the prejudice lingered, continuing to block minority families from many suburbs.

Banks and insurance companies also followed guidelines from the Federal Housing Administration (FHA) that favored racially homogenous neighborhoods—effectively shutting out Black, Latino, and Asian buyers from prime suburban tracts. As a result, middle-class minority families struggled to move into newly built areas, forcing them to remain in older districts or pay inflated prices in limited neighborhoods.

Consequences for Future Generations

These discriminatory policies created lasting wealth gaps. White families built home equity in the suburbs, passing resources to their children, while minority families often stayed in areas with lower property values and fewer public amenities. This pattern reinforced economic and racial divides across Los Angeles. Activists and civil rights organizations fought to end redlining and expand fair housing, but progress was slow. By the 1960s, the city's suburban ring was largely white, with many communities of color concentrated in the urban core or specific enclaves.

4. Golden Age of Hollywood

Studio Prosperity

In the 1950s, Hollywood enjoyed a brief "golden age" post-war. Big studios, though challenged by television's rise, still dominated film production. Epic spectacles, lavish musicals, and star-driven dramas enticed people into theaters. Stars like Marilyn Monroe, Elizabeth Taylor, and James Dean became cultural icons. Directors such as Cecil B. DeMille or Billy Wilder delivered blockbusters that showcased glossy sets and elaborate costumes. The Academy Awards, televised from 1953 onward, promoted Los Angeles as the glamorous capital of cinema.

Yet there were signs of trouble. Television chipped away at box-office receipts, and anti-monopoly rulings forced studios to sell off theater chains, weakening their vertical integration. Still, for many around the world, Hollywood symbolized the glitz and excitement of mid-century America. Tourists flocked to see celebrity homes and stroll down Hollywood Boulevard in hopes of spotting a star.

Television's Emergence

While overshadowed by movies at first, TV production soon took root in Los Angeles, especially in areas like Burbank or CBS Television City in the Fairfax District. Game shows, variety programs, and sitcoms found an eager audience. By the late 1950s, families who had previously gone to the movies every weekend were staying home for prime-time programs. Some film studios adapted by producing TV content or renting out soundstages to networks. This shift foreshadowed a broader diversification of Los Angeles' entertainment industry beyond the silver screen.

5. Rock and Roll and Youth Culture

New Music Scenes

The mid-century years saw the rise of **rock and roll**, igniting youth culture. Local radio stations, like KFWB and KRLA, played hits by Elvis Presley, Little Richard, and Chuck Berry. Teenage fans danced at sock hops or teen clubs, while parents and older generations sometimes disapproved of the "wild" rhythms. By the early 1960s, local bands sprang up, blending surf music (e.g., The Beach Boys) with rock, forging a distinct Southern California sound that celebrated beaches, cars, and sunshine.

Drive-In Restaurants and Car Culture

Los Angeles' love affair with the automobile extended to social spaces like **drive-in restaurants**. Teens cruised in hot rods or sporty convertibles, meeting up in parking lots for milkshakes and fries. Land along major boulevards became prime spots for car-centric businesses. The idea of "cruising the strip" was immortalized in movies and TV, further embedding L.A.'s reputation as a youthful, freewheeling city. These mid-century car rituals reflected both newfound prosperity and an emphasis on fun, though they exacerbated traffic congestion.

---

6. Disneyland and Theme Park Innovations

Walt Disney's Vision

In 1955, **Disneyland** opened in Anaheim, just southeast of downtown Los Angeles. Created by Walt Disney and his team of "Imagineers," the park combined fairy-tale castles, futuristic rides, and meticulously themed lands. Families from all over the country flocked to Disneyland, enjoying attractions like "Fantasyland," "Tomorrowland," and "Adventureland." This brand-new concept of a "theme park" was far more elaborate and immersive than older amusement parks. Disneyland quickly became a symbol of post-war optimism—clean, safe, and family-focused.

Economic Ripple Effects

The park's success spurred hotel construction, restaurants, and other tourist-related businesses in Orange County. Disneyland also influenced how future parks (like Knott's Berry Farm or Universal Studios tours) would develop. Urban planners took note of the traffic Disneyland generated, fueling more freeway expansions. Meanwhile, Los Angeles' image as a land of fantasy grew stronger, thanks to the synergy between Disneyland, Hollywood, and a public hungry for leisure experiences.

---

7. Water Expansion and the Metropolitan Water District

Seeking More Resources

As Los Angeles' population skyrocketed, local water supplies once again became a pressing issue. The Owens Valley aqueduct, built decades earlier, no longer sufficed. In 1931, the **Metropolitan Water District (MWD)** had formed to coordinate water development. By the 1950s, the MWD completed the **Colorado River Aqueduct**, bringing water from the Colorado River hundreds of miles away. This massive engineering feat included pumping stations, tunnels, and reservoirs, ensuring a stable supply for millions of new residents.

Environmental Costs

Tapping distant rivers had consequences. Owens Lake, already drained by the earlier aqueduct, remained a dusty expanse. The Colorado River's flow to its delta in Mexico diminished, affecting ecosystems and farmers downstream. Angelenos largely benefited from cheaper water, supporting lawns, swimming pools, and more farmland in the region. Critics warned of eventual limits to growth—could even the Colorado meet L.A.'s thirst forever? But mid-century leaders remained confident that engineering solutions could triumph over natural constraints.

8. Civil Rights Efforts

Black Community Activism

Though not as famous as movements in the South, Los Angeles had a robust **civil rights** movement by the 1950s. Organizations like the NAACP, the Urban League, and local church coalitions demanded fair housing and employment. African Americans faced housing covenants, police harassment, and school segregation in subtle forms. A landmark victory came with the **1954 Supreme Court decision Brown v. Board of Education**, inspiring activists to challenge Los Angeles Unified School District's de facto segregated schools.

Mexican American Organizing

Mexican American groups, including the Community Service Organization (CSO), fought discriminatory practices in education and jobs. Figures like Edward Roybal, elected to the City Council in 1949, represented East L.A. and championed minority rights in city government. He faced obstacles but opened doors for Latino politicians. Grassroots movements also demanded better conditions for farmworkers in the fields around Los Angeles County, foreshadowing Cesar Chavez's later statewide efforts.

---

9. Decline of Streetcars

End of the Red Cars

By the mid-1950s, the once-extensive Red Car system was in steep decline. Ridership dropped as families bought cars, and the private operators (Pacific Electric, etc.) lost money. City officials favored bus routes that used existing roads over funding track maintenance. Suburban sprawl left many areas unreachable by the old lines. In 1961, the final Red Car lines shut down, leaving only buses for mass transit. This closure signaled a definitive shift toward an auto-centric city, a hallmark of mid-century Los Angeles.

Missed Opportunities

Some urban planners argued that upgrading streetcars to modern light-rail or subways could ease congestion. But the political and financial climate favored freeways. As a result, Los Angeles drifted away from comprehensive public transit, a choice that would haunt the city in later decades when traffic jams and pollution became severe. Yet in the 1950s, few saw the immediate need for alternatives, believing cheap gas and open roads would suffice indefinitely.

10. Cold War Civil Defense

Fear of Nuclear Attack

With the Cold War escalating, Angelenos worried about a possible Soviet strike on the West Coast. Civil defense drills and pamphlets taught families to "duck and cover." Sirens tested monthly. Some homeowners built backyard fallout shelters, stocking them with canned goods and radios. Public buildings posted signs indicating "shelter" areas. The distinctive presence of aerospace factories and military bases in the region made Los Angeles feel like a prime target, even though no attacks occurred.

Aerospace Growth

Simultaneously, the aerospace industry thrived on Cold War defense contracts. Companies like Hughes Aircraft and RAND Corporation in Santa Monica developed missiles and scientific research. High-tech jobs attracted engineers and scientists from across the nation, raising the city's educational level. Local universities—UCLA, USC, and Caltech—benefited from federal grants and partnerships, training the workforce that fueled these advanced industries.

11. Cultural Shifts: Beat Generation and Modern Art

Beatniks and Counterculture

While mainstream culture embraced tract homes and suburban values, a bohemian undercurrent emerged in places like Venice Beach and along Sunset Strip. Writers, poets, and artists—some connected to the **Beat Generation**—challenged conservative norms. Coffeehouses featured poetry readings, jazz improvisations, and discussions about spirituality or politics. This scene overlapped with the city's earlier tradition of radical thought, but in a more artistic, introspective mode. By the early 1960s, these enclaves foreshadowed the coming youth rebellions of the later decade.

Modernist Architecture

Los Angeles also became a proving ground for **modernist architecture**, with sleek lines, large windows, and open floor plans. Architects like Richard Neutra and John Lautner designed futuristic homes that maximized light and views, especially on hillside lots. The famous "Case Study Houses" tested new materials and layouts. Although most middle-class families stuck to conventional ranch-style homes, these modernist experiments drew international attention, reinforcing L.A.'s image as a forward-looking metropolis.

---

12. Smog and Environmental Concerns

The Birth of Smog

As car usage skyrocketed, the Los Angeles basin—ringed by mountains—began experiencing severe air pollution known as **smog**. By the 1950s, thick brownish haze appeared, irritating eyes and lungs. Citizens complained of burning throats and decreased visibility. Scientists like Dr. Arie Haagen-Smit identified vehicle exhaust as a major culprit, reacting with sunlight to form ozone and other pollutants. This was a new phenomenon, not widely understood before.

Early Regulations

Alarmed city officials formed the Los Angeles Air Pollution Control District in 1947, one of the first agencies in the nation to tackle air quality. They pressured oil refineries and industrial plants to curb emissions. Automakers were slower to respond. California eventually led the way in requiring catalytic converters and other technologies, but these strict measures were still a few years off. Meanwhile, smog remained a daily annoyance and a health hazard, tarnishing the region's reputation for fresh air and sunshine.

---

13. Sports Franchises Arrive

Dodgers and Major League Baseball

In 1958, the Brooklyn Dodgers moved to Los Angeles, lured by a deal to build a modern stadium in Chavez Ravine. This move was controversial because it displaced a Mexican American community that lived on that hillside. Nonetheless, the arrival of the Dodgers signaled L.A.'s emergence as a major sports city. The team's immediate popularity soared, culminating in the opening of **Dodger Stadium** in 1962. Fans packed the stands to watch legendary players like Sandy Koufax and Don Drysdale, forging a new civic identity around baseball.

Lakers and the NBA

Around the same period, the Minneapolis Lakers relocated to Los Angeles in 1960. Though not as large a shock as the Dodgers' move, it confirmed the city's growing status as a magnet for big-time sports franchises. The Lakers soon became a powerhouse in professional basketball, and local fans flocked to the Los Angeles Memorial Sports Arena (later the Forum). These acquisitions of marquee teams helped unify the sprawling metropolis around shared sporting events and civic pride.

14. Downtown Development and Urban Renewal

High-Rises Begin to Appear

Mid-century Los Angeles saw the first signs of a modern downtown skyline. In the 1950s, building height restrictions dating back to the 1910s were relaxed. Though the city remained more horizontal than vertical, a few taller office structures rose along Wilshire Boulevard and near City Hall. Urban planners aimed to revitalize downtown, which had lost retail traffic to suburban malls. Projects like the **Bunker Hill redevelopment** started clearing older Victorian neighborhoods to make room for new offices, apartments, and cultural facilities.

Mixed Results

Advocates praised these efforts for attracting business and eliminating "blight." Critics argued that displacing low-income residents and demolishing historic buildings eroded the city's character. Bunker Hill, once full of grand old homes, became a vast construction site, with many families forced to move. Over time, this pattern repeated across other central areas. Some saw the transformations as necessary modernization; others lamented the loss of community fabric.

---

15. Police and City Politics

Chief William H. Parker and the LAPD

During the 1950s, **William H. Parker** served as Chief of the Los Angeles Police Department. He pushed for professionalizing the force, emphasizing discipline and modern crime-fighting techniques. Under Parker, the LAPD gained a reputation for efficiency, but also faced accusations of brutality, particularly in minority neighborhoods. Parker believed in strong control of the streets to combat perceived lawlessness, an approach that sometimes escalated tensions between police and communities of color.

City Hall Influence

Powerful figures like **Mayor Norris Poulson** (1953–1961) and later **Sam Yorty** (1961–1973) oversaw a mix of pro-business policies, freeway expansions, and downtown projects. They cultivated alliances with real estate developers and industry leaders. Meanwhile, grassroots activists struggled to have their voices heard, especially on issues like housing discrimination, public transit, and pollution. Los Angeles politics at mid-century balanced growth with public demands for fairness, though critics contended that growth usually won out.

16. Cultural Institutions and Pride

Music and Performing Arts

In the 1950s, the city's performing arts scene grew more prominent. The Los Angeles Philharmonic performed at the Hollywood Bowl each summer, delighting audiences with outdoor concerts. Opera and ballet companies matured, though they lacked a dedicated downtown venue until later decades. Jazz clubs along Central Avenue continued a rich tradition from earlier times, hosting legends like Charlie Parker, but faced declining attendance as tastes shifted to rock and pop.

Museums and Libraries

Art museums like the Los Angeles County Museum of History, Science, and Art (a precursor to LACMA) expanded their collections. Private collectors donated Western art, Spanish colonial artifacts, and modern pieces. The city also invested in libraries, though many branches were small or outdated. As suburban residents demanded cultural amenities closer to home, some wealthier enclaves started local arts councils or historical societies, preserving bits of local heritage amid rapid development.

17. Seeds of Future Unrest

Economic Disparities

While the white middle class thrived in suburban enclaves, many minority neighborhoods stagnated under discriminatory lending and poor public services. Youth in places like Watts felt disconnected from the city's prosperity. Underemployment, subpar schools, and limited city investment shaped a generation of frustration. Meanwhile, the LAPD's aggressive tactics exacerbated distrust in these communities.

Civil Rights Demonstrations

By the early 1960s, local activists staged peaceful protests at segregated restaurants or in front of real estate offices that refused minority buyers. Some black and Latino church leaders united to demand better policing and infrastructure. These efforts mirrored national movements for civil rights, though L.A. had unique patterns of sprawl and hidden discrimination. Observers sensed that unresolved tensions might erupt if conditions didn't improve. Indeed, this unrest foreshadowed the **Watts Riot** of 1965.

18. Environmental Awareness Grows

Smog Control Intensifies

As the 1960s began, smog remained a pressing concern. Scientists and local health officials urged stricter controls on industrial emissions and car exhaust. Civic groups lobbied for catalytic converters, alternative fuels, or mass transit solutions. Resistance came from car manufacturers, oil refineries, and free-market advocates who saw regulations as too burdensome. Nonetheless, a slow consensus formed that some regulation was needed to clear the skies. California's pioneering air pollution rules had their genesis here, setting a national precedent in later years.

Coastal Protection Movements

Development also threatened Los Angeles' beaches. In places like Malibu, real estate deals sealed off public access to the shore. Environmentalists formed early coalitions to preserve beaches and wetlands from being turned into private marinas or highways. State and local governments began discussing "coastal zone" regulations to balance economic use with public interest. This marked a new phase in environmental activism, beyond just smog or water issues, shaping the city's relationship with its coastline.

19. National Politics and Los Angeles' Role

Eisenhower Years to Kennedy

During Dwight D. Eisenhower's presidency (1953–1961), federal funds continued to flow into Southern California for highways and aerospace. Under John F. Kennedy, the **space race** ramped up, boosting NASA-related work in the region. Los Angeles engineers and scientists contributed to missile and rocket designs, culminating in local involvement in the Apollo program. This synergy of national priorities and local expertise propelled the city's mid-century prestige as a technological and cultural center.

Influence on Pop Culture

Los Angeles, through Hollywood, shaped national attitudes about suburbs, cars, and youth. TV shows like "Leave It to Beaver" or "The Adventures of Ozzie and Harriet," often filmed or set in Southern California, portrayed an idealized suburban life. Advertisements showcased sleek mid-century furniture and modern kitchen appliances, echoing the region's design ethos. Thus, Los Angeles exported an image of carefree affluence to the rest of the country, sometimes glossing over the inequalities within its own borders.

CHAPTER 20

The Path Toward Modern Times

The 1960s and early 1970s represented both turmoil and innovation for Los Angeles. While post-war optimism fueled suburban sprawl and booming industries, it became clear that deep social divisions remained. This period saw major civil unrest, public protests, changes in urban policy, and the rise of new cultural forces. By the mid-1970s, Los Angeles had entered a new phase, bridging the older patterns we have traced throughout this book into the outlines of the modern megacity we know today. In this final chapter, we look at pivotal events like the **Watts Riot**, continued freeway expansions, the Chicano Movement, environmental milestones, and the shifting cultural landscape that led Los Angeles from its deep past into the threshold of the modern era.

1. Watts Riot (1965)

Underlying Causes

Decades of housing discrimination, poor schools, and harsh policing set the stage for an explosive event in **Watts**, a predominantly African American neighborhood in South Los Angeles. Unemployment and substandard services eroded trust in local government. Many residents felt the city's prosperity bypassed them, as suburban growth and new freeways seemed to benefit wealthier, largely white areas. Tensions with the LAPD, which had a reputation for aggressive tactics under Chief William H. Parker, were especially high.

Spark and Outcome

On August 11, 1965, a minor traffic stop escalated into a confrontation between police and bystanders. Rumors of police brutality spread quickly, triggering days of rioting, looting, and violence. The National Guard was called in to restore order. Over 30 people died, hundreds were injured, and property damage reached tens of millions of dollars. The Watts Riot was the worst urban disturbance in Los Angeles history up to that point, shocking the nation and drawing attention to systemic racism. Post-riot commissions recommended reforms—improved housing, job programs, and better police-community relations—but actual progress proved slow.

2. Aftermath and Political Shifts

Mayor Sam Yorty and Beyond

Mayor **Sam Yorty** (1961–1973) struggled to address the complex fallout of the Watts Riot. Although he commissioned studies and advocated for certain anti-poverty measures, critics felt his approach was too narrow. He also clashed with the city's African American community and liberal voices calling for deeper structural changes. By the 1970s, a new generation of leaders began rising, promising a more inclusive vision.

Tom Bradley's Emergence

One of the most significant figures to emerge was **Tom Bradley**, an African American city councilman and former LAPD officer. Elected to the City Council in 1963, Bradley challenged Yorty in the 1969 mayoral race but narrowly lost. However, he built alliances with various ethnic communities and middle-class liberals across the city. In 1973, Bradley would finally become mayor, symbolizing a transition in Los Angeles politics that sought to address racial inequalities and modernize city governance.

3. The Chicano Movement

East L.A. Activism

The **Chicano Movement**, which took shape in the 1960s, demanded better education, political representation, and cultural pride for Mexican Americans. East Los Angeles became a hub of student walkouts, known as the **Blowouts** (1968), where high school students protested underfunded, overcrowded schools. Activists like Sal Castro and groups like the Brown Berets championed community empowerment and an end to discriminatory practices. They confronted police harassment, unfair tracking in schools, and limited job opportunities.

Cultural Renaissance

Beyond protests, the movement sparked a cultural renaissance in art, music, and literature. Murals depicting Chicano heritage, indigenous symbols, and social themes appeared on walls throughout East L.A. Musicians blended rock, soul, and traditional Mexican sounds, forging new styles that resonated with youth. Theater groups performed bilingual plays highlighting immigrant struggles. This assertive embrace of identity pushed Los Angeles to reckon with its large Latino population as more than just labor; it was a community with rich history and demands for equity.

---

4. Continuing Freeway Expansions

Freeway Construction and Public Pushback

Through the 1960s, freeways multiplied, including segments of the **San Diego Freeway (I-405)**, the **Santa Monica Freeway (I-10)**, and the **San Bernardino Freeway (I-10)** through East L.A. But unlike the 1950s, some neighborhoods organized resistance. Communities rallied to block freeways from bulldozing stable areas, citing earlier examples of displacement. Environmental concerns grew too—people worried about noise, smog, and the division of neighborhoods. While some routes proceeded, others stalled or were canceled, marking a shift from unquestioned freeway building to a more contested process.

The Birth of a Freeway Culture

Still, the majority of Angelenos continued to rely on cars, and suburban job centers emerged. Malls anchored by large parking lots sprouted off freeway exits, furthering the region's decentralized sprawl. Traffic congestion became a daily reality, leading local media to highlight "carmageddon" scenarios. Calls for improved public transit surfaced, but no major rail system advanced in these years, as political will and funding were lacking. The city thus doubled down on freeway dependency, shaping its identity as the car capital of America.

5. Environmental Milestones

Air Quality Regulation

Smog levels kept rising through the 1960s, prompting stronger local and state rules. In 1967, California formed the **Air Resources Board**, tasked with developing statewide controls on vehicle emissions. This led to the first tailpipe regulations that forced automakers to introduce emission-reducing technologies. Over time, smog checks, unleaded gasoline, and catalytic converters would help, though progress was gradual. Los Angeles took pride in pioneering these measures, even as many drivers grumbled about increased costs.

Santa Barbara Oil Spill and Coastal Movements

In 1969, a major oil spill off the coast of Santa Barbara (north of L.A. County) shocked Californians. While not in Los Angeles itself, it galvanized environmental groups statewide to demand stricter controls on offshore drilling. L.A.'s coastal communities joined in calling for better protection of beaches, wildlife, and wetlands. This momentum contributed to future legislation like the 1972 Coastal Act, which shaped development along the entire California coast.

6. Rise of Counterculture and Music Scenes

Sunset Strip and the Hippie Influence

By the mid-1960s, Los Angeles saw a wave of counterculture energy, especially in neighborhoods near the **Sunset Strip** in West Hollywood. Teen clubs hosted rock bands like The Doors, Buffalo Springfield, and Love, fusing psychedelic and folk influences. Hippies with long hair and tie-dye clothes mingled with celebrities and locals. Clubs like the Whisky a Go Go became launching pads for new sounds. The local "flower power" vibe blended with the city's earlier beatnik enclaves, creating a lively, experimental youth culture.

Protests and Gatherings

The **Vietnam War** fueled widespread protests. College campuses—UCLA, Cal State L.A., and smaller community colleges—organized anti-war marches, teach-ins, and sit-ins. Young people questioned government policies, police actions, and the draft. This activism intertwined with civil rights and Chicano demonstrations, forging alliances around anti-establishment sentiment. The police often responded with strong tactics, raising tensions. Los Angeles thus became a stage for the same youthful unrest that swept much of the nation, but with its own West Coast flair.

7. Changing Face of Hollywood

New Hollywood Filmmakers

The film industry in the 1960s grappled with competition from television and evolving audience tastes. Some old-school studio heads retired, replaced by younger executives open to riskier projects. A wave of **New Hollywood** directors—Francis Ford Coppola, Peter Bogdanovich, and others—experimented with more personal, edgy films. While many shot on location outside L.A., the city's studios remained key production centers, adjusting to modern times. Box-office hits like "The Sound of Music" (1965) showed big musicals still had an audience, but more daring films signaled a cultural shift.

TV Production Expands

Television kept growing, with new sitcoms, dramas, and variety shows produced in Burbank, Studio City, and Culver City. Networks established permanent facilities, employing hundreds of technicians. Popular programs like "The Beverly Hillbillies," "Dragnet," and "The Lucy Show" were taped or filmed locally. This synergy between TV and film expanded the entertainment job market, even as the city's population soared. Tourists increasingly wanted to see TV tapings, prompting studios to offer limited audience tickets, adding another dimension to the tourist economy.

8. Police Reform and Continued Tensions

LAPD in the Wake of Watts

After the Watts Riot, calls for police reform intensified. The Civil Rights Commission, community leaders, and some politicians urged the LAPD to recruit more minority officers and adopt less confrontational methods. Chief Parker died in 1966, succeeded by **Thomas Reddin** and later **Edward M. Davis**, both of whom maintained a strong law-and-order approach. While minor changes occurred, many Black and Latino residents still reported discriminatory stops and rough treatment.

The Charles Manson Murders

In 1969, a series of grisly killings by the **Manson Family** targeted high-profile residents in the Hollywood Hills (including actress Sharon Tate). This crime spree gripped national headlines and cast a dark shadow over the city's freewheeling counterculture. It prompted concerns about cults, drug abuse, and the perceived breakdown of moral order. The LAPD's handling of the case eventually led to Manson's arrest and trial, but the sensationalist media coverage stoked fear that the city's laid-back hippie ethos masked lurking dangers.

9. Downtown Revitalization Efforts

Music Center and Civic Redevelopment

While suburbanization continued, city leaders sought to keep downtown relevant. The **Music Center**—including the Dorothy Chandler Pavilion and

Mark Taper Forum—opened in the mid-1960s, aiming to anchor a high-culture district near Bunker Hill. This project replaced older neighborhoods with modern structures, parks, and fountains. Critics lamented the loss of historic buildings, but supporters hailed it as proof Los Angeles was a global city worthy of top-tier cultural venues.

Corporate Towers

By the late 1960s, corporate headquarters and banks financed new skyscrapers. Land was cleared for parking structures and wide boulevards. Downtown Los Angeles, once overshadowed by the Hollywood and Wilshire corridors, began forging a new identity as a vertical business center. However, after-hours activity remained limited, as many employees commuted back to the suburbs. The city's multiple "downtowns"—Century City, Glendale, and other business hubs—reflected its decentralized nature.

---

10. The Emergence of Neighborhood Councils

Grassroots Participation

In response to rapid changes and top-down projects (like freeways or redevelopment bulldozing), more neighborhoods formed councils or associations. They wanted a voice in city decisions on zoning, public works, and policing. Some councils represented middle-class homeowners protecting property values; others, in working-class or minority areas, pushed for better schools, parks, and street lighting. This grassroots activism marked a shift from trusting city hall to handle everything toward community-based planning.

Early Wins and Ongoing Struggles

A few councils succeeded in blocking or modifying proposed freeway routes. Others lobbied for new libraries or community centers. Yet real power remained with the mayor and city council, who often listened more to business interests. Over time, these local groups laid foundations for the official neighborhood council system that would emerge in the 1990s. In the 1960s-70s, their impact was modest, but they signaled a new wave of citizen engagement in local government.

11. UCLA, USC, and Student Movements

Campus Activism

Los Angeles' major universities, particularly **UCLA** and **USC**, became hotbeds of social engagement during the 1960s. Students protested the Vietnam War, formed civil rights clubs, and hosted teach-ins about racism, sexism, and globalization. Administrators grappled with demands to diversify faculty and curricula, while police occasionally clashed with demonstrators. These movements connected to national trends, but also mirrored local issues like housing discrimination or police conduct.

Intellectual Growth

Despite turmoil, the universities expanded. New buildings, research grants, and faculty hires elevated their academic reputations. UCLA's film school gained fame as a center for young filmmakers, including some from minority backgrounds who would later shape Hollywood. USC's engineering and communications departments thrived with corporate partnerships. These campuses, along with community colleges, would help power L.A.'s future by producing skilled graduates in technology, arts, and public service.

---

12. Changing Racial Dynamics in Suburbs

African American Migration to the Valley

As the civil rights movement progressed, a few Black families gained access to suburban tracts in the San Fernando Valley. They faced hostility from some neighbors, but fair housing laws and court decisions slowly chipped away at segregation. This allowed a small but growing Black middle class to settle beyond the traditional boundaries of South Central. Similar patterns emerged for Mexican Americans moving into Eastside suburbs. While the pace of integration was slow, it hinted at a future where Los Angeles' diversity would spread across more regions.

White Flight and Re-Segregation

In some older suburbs, white families moved farther out once minorities arrived—so-called "white flight." This created new rings of development in places like the Santa Clarita Valley or Orange County, leaving behind transitional neighborhoods in the inner ring. School districts faced complex busing controversies to achieve racial balance. Debates about property values, local control, and discrimination flared in city council meetings and courtrooms, shaping L.A.'s educational landscape for decades.

---

13. The 1970 Chicano Moratorium

Anti-War Protest

By 1970, the Vietnam War remained divisive. Mexican American activists organized the **Chicano Moratorium**, a mass protest in East L.A. condemning high casualty rates of Latino soldiers in the war, as well as broader social injustices at home. Thousands marched peacefully on August 29, 1970. Tensions with sheriff's deputies escalated, leading to clashes and arrests. Notably, journalist **Ruben Salazar** was killed by a tear gas projectile in a nearby bar, becoming a martyr for the movement.

Lasting Impact

The Chicano Moratorium underscored how Latino communities linked foreign policy critiques to local civil rights struggles. Salazar's death spurred demands for accountability and reform in law enforcement. Though the immediate outcome was tragic, many who participated or witnessed the protest felt galvanized to continue organizing. This event stands as a key moment in Los Angeles' Latino history, demonstrating the community's capacity for large-scale political action.

---

14. Cultural Institutions Blossom

LA County Museum of Art (LACMA)

Opened in 1965 on Wilshire Boulevard's Miracle Mile, **LACMA** marked a major step in the city's artistic profile. Freed from the older Exposition Park site, the museum curated ambitious exhibits, bringing global art movements to local audiences. Wealthy donors contributed private collections, raising the museum's stature. LACMA soon became a cultural anchor, spurring neighboring expansions like the Page Museum at the La Brea Tar Pits. Meanwhile, contemporary art galleries flourished around the city, reflecting rising interest in modern and pop art.

Music and Theater Scenes

Downtown's Music Center—Dorothy Chandler Pavilion, Mark Taper Forum, and Ahmanson Theatre—brought high-profile opera, symphony, and stage productions. Meanwhile, smaller venues around Hollywood staged experimental theater and rock concerts. From folk clubs on the Westside to jazz spots in Leimert Park, Los Angeles' mid-century music scene diversified. By the 1970s, the city hosted everything from symphonic masterworks to the roots of punk rock, showcasing an eclectic cultural mosaic.

---

15. Tech and Aerospace Evolution

The Space Race Boost

The Apollo program, culminating in the Moon landing of 1969, drew heavily on Los Angeles' aerospace expertise. Firms like North American Rockwell (formerly North American Aviation) built Saturn V rocket stages. Thousands of engineers and technicians in the region contributed, forging solutions that advanced electronics, materials science, and computing. This synergy led to spin-off tech companies focusing on everything from early microchips to advanced communications.

Post-Apollo Shifts

When NASA scaled back moon missions in the early 1970s, local aerospace jobs waned slightly. Yet the city still maintained a broad defense industrial base, pivoting to satellites, missile systems, and commercial aviation. Universities like Caltech and UCLA, working with the Jet Propulsion Laboratory in Pasadena, fueled planetary research and robotics. Though overshadowed by future Silicon Valley, mid-century L.A. laid crucial groundwork for the digital revolution.

---

16. Reevaluating Urban Policies

Growing Critiques of Sprawl

By the early 1970s, some urban planners and intellectuals criticized Los Angeles' sprawl. They cited endless commutes, air pollution, and the destruction of farmland and open space. Environmentalists proposed "smart growth" strategies, preserving greenbelts and encouraging higher-density housing near transit corridors. However, the city's longstanding preference for single-family zoning and car-centric planning proved resistant to change. Most local governments in the region still favored continued outward development, aligning with homeowner interests.

Early Transit Proposals

Civic groups revisited the idea of a rail network or subway system to alleviate traffic. A 1968 referendum to fund a modern rail line failed amid concerns about cost and skepticism from car-loving Angelenos. Without broad public buy-in, the city stuck to building more freeways and widening roads. Hints of future changes appeared, such as experimental busways or dedicated lanes, but a comprehensive approach to mass transit would not fully materialize until the 1980s and beyond.

17. Tom Bradley's Victory in 1973

The First African American Mayor

In 1973, **Tom Bradley** was elected mayor, defeating Sam Yorty in a political upset. Bradley, a moderate Democrat, built a coalition of Black voters, Latinos, liberal whites, and business leaders disillusioned with Yorty's style. His victory signaled that Los Angeles was ready for more inclusive leadership. Bradley promised to tackle racial inequities, improve public transit, and foster economic growth. His tenure would last five terms (1973–1993), shaping the city's modern identity.

Bridging Past and Future

Though Bradley's administration extended beyond this chapter's primary time frame, his win marks a symbolic closing of an older political era and the opening of a new one—where a multiethnic coalition could guide city policy. Bradley's approach balanced progressive aims (expanding city services, civil rights) with pro-business stances (attracting corporate headquarters, planning major events like the 1984 Olympics). This dual strategy exemplified Los Angeles' complexity at the threshold of modern times.

---

18. The End of an Era for Old Landmarks

Victorian and Streetcar Suburbs

Many older areas faced demolition or renovation. Bunker Hill's Victorian mansions were cleared for modern towers. Streetcar-era neighborhoods, built around now-defunct lines, either declined or adapted to new uses. Preservationists struggled to save historic structures, but laws protecting older buildings were weak. By the mid-1970s, pockets of Victorian or Craftsman charm remained in places like Angelino Heights or Pasadena, but the city's overall face had changed drastically from even a few decades earlier.

Shifts in Agriculture

In the outlying valleys, orange groves and vineyards gave way to suburban streets, industrial parks, and commercial strips. The "Orange Empire" that once defined Los Angeles County agriculture retreated to remote corners. Some wealthier enclaves maintained equestrian zones or decorative lemon trees, but the age of large-scale orchard farming near the city was over, replaced by housing tracts and shopping malls.

---

19. Cultural Crossroads: Looking Ahead

Legacy of the 1960s Movements

The activism of African Americans, Mexican Americans, and other groups in the 1960s laid foundations for later reforms. Laws banning housing discrimination and guaranteeing bilingual education emerged, though enforcement varied. The cross-cultural alliances formed during protests provided a roadmap for future campaigns, shaping city politics in the decades to come. While prejudice and inequality persisted, Los Angeles could no longer ignore the demands of its diverse populace.

Evolving Identity

By the early 1970s, Los Angeles was recognized as a global city—home to Hollywood, major sports teams, world-class museums, an aerospace powerhouse, and rising political figures. Yet it also carried the burdens of traffic congestion, smog, racial tensions, and uneven development. The city's identity as a sunny paradise coexisted with deeper social complexities. Observers predicted that if L.A. could solve these challenges, it might offer a model for other urban regions worldwide.

---

20. Conclusion: Bridging the Past to the Present

Throughout these final decades we have examined—roughly the 1960s into the early 1970s—Los Angeles took critical steps **toward modern times**:

1. **Civil Unrest:** The Watts Riot (1965) revealed deep-rooted racial injustices, prompting calls for reforms that began but were not fully realized.

2. **Political Shifts:** Emerging leaders like Tom Bradley signaled a more inclusive governance, reflecting the city's changing demographics.

3. **Social Movements:** The Chicano Movement, anti-war protests, and counterculture shaped youth identity and broadened civic engagement.

4. **Freeway Overdrive:** Construction continued, though citizens increasingly questioned the costs of endless car-centric development.

5. **Environmental Awakening:** Smog laws, coastal protection, and growing ecology awareness sowed seeds of policy that would later define L.A.'s approach to sustainability.

6. **Cultural Fusion:** Los Angeles saw a blend of new music, film innovation, and multicultural art forms that made it an epicenter of creativity.

7. **From Old to New:** The bulldozing of older districts and farmland signaled a final break with the city's agricultural and low-rise heritage, ushering in the era of high-rises, suburban sprawl, and mega-development.

By the mid-1970s, Los Angeles was poised on the edge of yet another wave of transformations—global migration, advanced technology, expanding suburbs, and new cultural expressions. The threads of older history, from the Spanish pueblo to the mission era, from ranchos to railroads, from the oil and film booms to the WWII defense economy, all connected here. The city's story after the 1970s is one of further growth, challenges, and cultural evolution, but that extends into more modern times, beyond the scope of our focused historical narrative.

We end our journey with Los Angeles at a crossroads between the old and the new. Its past is filled with triumphs, conflicts, and remarkable achievements—prehistoric lands, indigenous tribes, Spanish colonial rule, Mexican governance, American conquest, ranchos, missions, gold rush, railroads, agriculture, oil, Hollywood, war industries, suburban sprawl, civil rights struggles, and budding environmental consciousness. All these elements make Los Angeles a unique tapestry of cultures and landscapes, an ever-evolving city that still bears the marks of its long and complex history.

With this final chapter, we have traced Los Angeles from its earliest times through to the threshold of the modern era. The city's future developments—post-1970s—would continue in the same spirit of reinvention, forging the global metropolis we know today. Yet the foundations, tensions, and legacies we have explored remain vital to understanding how Los Angeles became what it is: a place of dreams and challenges, sunshine and smog, unity and division, forever shaped by the layers of its past.

Help Us Share Your Thoughts!

Dear reader,

Thank you for spending your time with this book. We hope it brought you enjoyment and a few new ideas to think about. If there was anything that didn't work for you, or if you have suggestions on how we can improve, please let us know at **kontakt@skriuwer.com**. Your feedback means a lot to us and helps us make our books even better.

If you enjoyed this book, we would be very grateful if you left a review on the site where you purchased it. Your review not only helps other readers find our books, but also encourages us to keep creating more stories and materials that you'll love.

By choosing Skriuwer, you're also supporting **Frisian**—a minority language mainly spoken in the northern Netherlands. Although **Frisian** has a rich history, the number of speakers is shrinking, and it's at risk of dying out. Your purchase helps fund resources to preserve and promote this language, such as educational programs and learning tools. If you'd like to learn more about Frisian or even start learning it yourself, please visit **www.learnfrisian.com**.

Thank you for being part of our community. We look forward to sharing more books with you in the future.

Warm regards,
The Skriuwer Team

www.ingramcontent.com/pod-product-compliance
Lightning Source LLC
LaVergne TN
LVHW012036070526
838202LV00056B/5517